THEMATIC UNIT
EXPLORERS

Written By Mary Ellen Sterling
Illustrated by Cheryl Buhler

Teacher Created Materials, Inc.
6421 Industry Way
Westminster, CA 92683
www.teachercreated.com
©1992 Teacher Created Materials, Inc.
Reprinted, 2003
Made in U.S.A.
ISBN-1-55734-288-1

Table of Contents

Introduction

Explorers contains a captivating, whole language, thematic unit about the Age of Exploration. Its 80 exciting pages are filled with a wide variety of lesson ideas and reproducibles designed for use with intermediate and junior high school children. At its core are two high-quality children's literature selections, *The Log of Christopher Columbus' First Voyage to America* and *The Usborne Book of Explorers*. For each of these books, activities are included which set the stage for reading, encourage the enjoyment of the book, and extend the concepts gained. In addition, the theme is connected to the curriculum with activities in language arts (including writing suggestions), math, science, social studies, art, music, and life skills (cooking, etc.). Many of these activities encourage cooperative learning. Suggestions for bulletin boards are additional time savers for the busy teacher. Furthermore, directions for student-created Big Books and culminating activities, which allow students to synthesize their knowledge in order to produce products that can be shared beyond the classroom, highlight this very complete teacher resource.

This thematic unit includes:

- ❑ **literature selections**—summaries of two children's books with related lessons (complete with reproducible pages that cross the curriculum)

- ❑ **poetry and drama**—suggested selections and lessons enabling students to act out and create their own stories

- ❑ **writing ideas**—daily suggestions as well as activities across the curriculum, including Big Books

- ❑ **bulletin board ideas**—suggestions and plans for student-created and/or interactive bulletin boards

- ❑ **homework suggestions**—extending the unit to the child's home

- ❑ **curriculum connections**—in language arts, math, science, social studies, art, music, and life skills

- ❑ **group projects**—to foster cooperative learning

- ❑ **a bibliography**—suggesting additional books on the theme

---

To keep this valuable resource intact so that it can be used year after year, you may wish to punch holes in the pages and store them in a three-ring binder.

Introduction *(Cont.)*

Why Whole Language?

A whole language approach involves children in using all modes of communications: reading, writing, listening, observing, illustrating, experiencing, and doing. Communication skills are interconnected and integrated into lessons that emphasize the whole of language rather than isolating its parts. The lessons revolve around selected literature. Reading is not taught as a separate subject from writing and spelling, for example. A child reads, writes (spelling appropriately for his/her level), speaks, listens, etc. in response to a literature experience introduced by the teacher. In this way, language skills grow naturally, stimulated by involvement and interest in the topic at hand.

Why Thematic Planning?

One very useful tool for implementing an integrated whole language program is thematic planning. By choosing a theme with correlating literature selections for a unit of study, a teacher can plan activities throughout the day that lead to a cohesive, in-depth study of the topic. Students will be practicing and applying their skills in meaningful contexts. Consequently, they will tend to learn and retain more. Both teachers and students will be freed from a day that is broken into unrelated segments of isolated drill and practice.

Why Cooperative Learning?

Beside academic skills and content, students need to learn social skills. No longer can this area of development be taken for granted. Students must learn to work cooperatively in groups in order to function well in modern society. Group activities should be a regular part of school life and teachers should consciously include social objectives as well as academic objectives in their planning. For example, a group working together to write a report may need to select a leader. The teacher should make clear to the students and monitor the qualities of good leader-follower group interaction just as he/ she would state and monitor the academic goals of the project.

Why Big Books?

An excellent cooperative, whole language activity is the production of Big Books. Groups of students, or the whole class, can apply their language skills, content knowledge, and creativity to produce a Big Book that can become a part of the classroom library to be read and reread. These books make excellent culminating projects for sharing beyond the classroom with parents, librarians, other classes, etc. Big Books can be produced in many ways, and this thematic unit book includes directions for at least one method you may choose.

The Log of Christopher Columbus' First Voyage to America

Summary

When Columbus' fleet set sail from Palos, Spain, for the Indies on Friday August 3, 1492, they did so with the intentions of claiming the land for Spain, converting the natives to Catholicism, and bringing back gold and riches for King Ferdinand and Queen Isabella. Since the waters were virtually uncharted, no one knew with certainty what adventures were to befall the crew This diary gives us a firsthand account of what those days were like. It tells of the disenchantment among the men as they sailed longer and longer without seeing land. It gives the reader insight into the misguided beliefs about sea travel that were commonly thought to be true at the time.

The passages contained in the book are taken from the actual journal of Bartholomew Las Casas, Columbus' traveling companion. Included on the pages are accurate pictorial footnotes from the log. Among the drawings are the three sailing vessels, navigational tools, and marine life. This book brings history alive and gives the reader an eyewitness look at one of the most important events in the history of mankind.

The outline below is a suggested plan for using the various activities that are presented in this unit. You should adapt these ideas to fit your own classroom situation.

Sample Plan

Day I

- Compare and contrast current maps with Toscanelli's chart (page 9)
- Discuss fears of early sailors
- Construct a web of reasons for exploration
- Sailing technology: Nautical Help Worksheet (page 10)

Day II

- Begin ongoing chart (see #5, page 6)
- Knowledge Activity. Know the Facts (page 11)
- Vocabulary: Match Up (page 12)
- Mapping Columbus' Route (page 13)

Day III

- Draw the Green Cross (page 14)
- Comprehension Game (page 15)
- Character Traits (page 16)
- Creative Writing Projects (pages 17 & 18)
- Math Word Problems (pages 19 and 20)
- Constellations background information (page 21)

Day IV

- Meteors and comets worksheet (page 22)
- Latitude and longitude review (page 23)
- Voyage to the Indies Game (pages 24 - 25)
- Science Projects (page 26)
- Three art ideas (page 27)

Day V

- Construct Time Lines (see #1, page 8)
- Explorer newspaper Big Book idea (page 8)
- Explorer s Picnic (page 29)
- Write Diaries (see #4, page 8)

Overview of Activities

SETTING THE STAGE

1. **Compare maps.** Divide the students into small groups. Provide each group with a map of the world (an atlas is a good resource) and a copy of Toscanelli's chart (see page 9). Direct the students to find the West Indies and the Americas on the current map and then on the ancient map. Ask why they think both the Indies and the Americas are missing from Toscanelli's chart. Discuss several possibilities. Observe other discrepancies - Africa, the North and South Poles, etc.

2. **Chart reasons for fears.** Help students understand that although the lands always existed, they were unknown to one another. Tell them why people were afraid to explore. Some thought the world was flat, and it was possible to sail off the edge of the earth. Others feared there were monsters in the sea or that the waters near the equator were boiling hot. Talk about other reasons sailors were reluctant to explore unknown waters. Make a chart of these reasons.

3. **Web of reasons for explorations.** Brainstorm with the students the reasons for exploration in the 1400's. Make a web of all possible explorations. Students may need to use resource books for this activity; see the Bibliography, page 80, for suggested titles.

Spices, silks, gems
Crusades took them there
Better technology
Reasons for Exploration
Learned by Asia's riches by reading
Way to spread Christianity

4. **Discuss the advances made in sailing technology.** Have the students complete the Nautical Help Worksheet on page 10. As a class, review the correct responses.

What We Know	What We Learned
1. Columbus sailed from Spain	1. Native Americans were treated cruelly

5. **What we learned.** Find out what the students already know about Columbus' voyage. Write the responses on one half of a chart. On the other half write the title, "What We Learned." Add to it throughout the unit. Display the chart so that it is highly visible. The information can be used in writing assignments or for the construction of assessment tools (true/false questions, essay questions, etc.).

ENJOYING THE BOOK

1. **Read aloud.** Have the students read *The Log of Christopher Columbus' First Voyage to America*. Notice that some dates have been omitted and that some entries are longer than others. Discuss possible reasons for this.

2. **Knowledge Activity.** Have pairs or individuals complete the Know the Facts worksheet on page 11. As an alternative, write the answers from the Word Bank on the chalkboard or overhead projector. Read a description and have the students identify the correct answer. This may be used as an oral review or assessment of the student's knowledge.

3. **Word Knowledge.** Pair the students. Have them copy the words from the Word Box (see page 12) and define each one. Follow up with the Match Up activity on the same page.

Overview of Activities *(cont.)*

ENJOYING THE BOOK *(cont.)*

4. **Columbus' Route.** Have the students trace Columbus' route to the West Indies. The worksheet on page 13 also requires labeling of various lands along the way. Students may refer to *The Log of Christopher Columbus' First Voyage to America* if needed.

5. Mental Pictures. Read the description of the Green Cross from the Friday, October 12, 1492 entry. Have student volunteers draw pictures of the flag, based on the verbal description, on the chalkboard. Display the illustration from the book and compare. All students can participate by completing the worksheet on page 14.

6. **Comprehension Game.** Groups compete for points in the game found on page 15. As they play, have the groups record their responses. Later, review the questions as a class.

7. **Character Traits.** Discuss character traits with the students. Establish the fact that everyone has strong and weak traits. On the chalkboard, overhead projector, or chart paper make a list of what students consider their strong points and another list of what they consider to be their weaknesses. Have them explain their reasoning. Now talk about Columbus' strong and weak traits. For example, Columbus was optimistic. During the voyage he knew they couldn't be far from land because of the various animal and physical signs (whales, berry branches, cloud banks, etc.). Find out about other traits by completing the worksheet on page 16.

Strong	Weak
Persistent- always finish my projects even if they are hard to do	**Easily distracted -** if the TV is on, I watch it instead of doing my studies

8. **Creative Writing.** The ideas presented on page 17 and 18 can be used in a number of ways. Several alternatives are listed for your use.

9. **Math.** Many math word problems can be developed from the information given throughout Columbus' log. The Math on Board worksheet on page 19 contains a sample of possible problems. Pairs of students can work together on this activity.

$C = \pi r^2$

10. **More Math.** Students will learn some interesting facts about Columbus' voyage when they work their way through this worksheet on page 20. As an extension activity, learn about circumference and the formula used to find circumference.

11. **Constellations.** Heighten student interest in the stars with this worksheet on page 21. Have the students work in groups to complete one of the On Your Own Projects. When their writing and reports are done, have them give oral presentations to the whole group. If possible, plan a field trip to a planetarium or go star-gazing one evening.

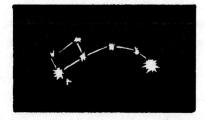

12. **Meteors and Comets.** An interesting duo of phenomena for students to explore are meteors and comets. Learn all about their differences on page 22.

Overview of Activities *(cont.)*

ENJOYING THE BOOK *(cont.)*

13. **Geography Skills.** Review latitude and longitude by reading the paragraph and labeling the diagram on page 23. As a follow-up activity, encourage the students to find the lines on an actual globe. Then to help students conceptualize directions, prepare one or more Voyage to the Indies gameboards (pages 24 and 25). Students may play this game during free time or a designated time period.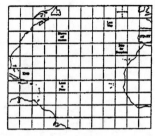

14. **Science.** Quick, fun, easy-to-prepare science projects are described on page 26. They are most effective when students can complete them on their own, but they may be presented as demonstrations by the teacher.

15. **Art.** Art Works on page 27 describes three projects that can be coordinated with the daily lesson plans and easily incorporated into a culminating activity.

EXTENDING THE BOOK

1. **Construct Time Lines** of other explorers and famous people who were alive at the time of Columbus. Write the name and birth date of each person on an index card. In one or two sentences tell about their greatest accomplishments. When all the cards are complete, line them up on a chalk tray or paper clip them to a yarn line. An excellent resource for this activity is Christas Kondeatis' *The Junior Wall Chart of History* (Barnes and Noble, 1990) which unfolds into a six-foot long chart of people, places, and events.

2. **Big Book Idea.** Create a newspaper that chronicles Columbus and his time. Assign different articles to groups of students or individuals. Include news reports, an editorial, a feature story, classified ads, comics, world news, letters to the editor, and an activity page. You may wish to review newspaper article writing with the worksheet on page 28. For more and complete directions about newspaper writing use Teacher Created Materials #137 *Newspaper Reporters*. Newspaper outlines (#138) are also available through Teacher Created Materials.

3. **Explorer's Picnic.** In this culminating activity (see pages 29 and 30) students will experience life on board the *Santa Maria,* write letters home, eat sea rations, and play a game called Shipwrecked. Forms for letter-writing and journal entries are included.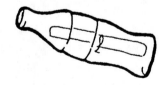

4. **Diaries.** *The Log of Christopher Columbus' First Voyage to America* is written in a diary format. Have students read another book written in a similar style. Two good resources for this activity follow: *Three Days on a River in a Red Canoe* by Vera B. Williams (Mulberry Books, 1981) and *Stringbean's Trip to the Shining Sea* also by Vera B. Williams (Greenwillow, 1988). Direct the students to keep a one-week diary or journal on an imaginary journey of their choice.

Toscanelli's Chart

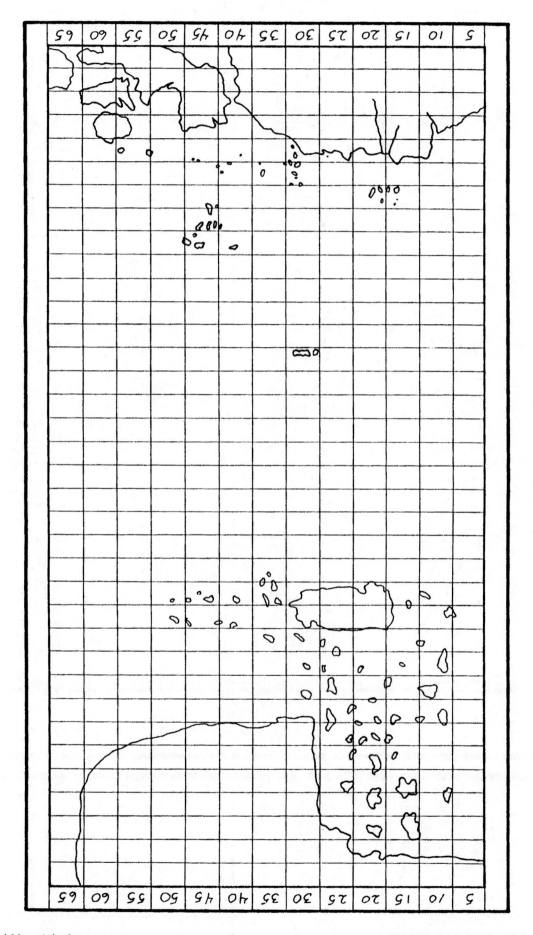

Nautical Help

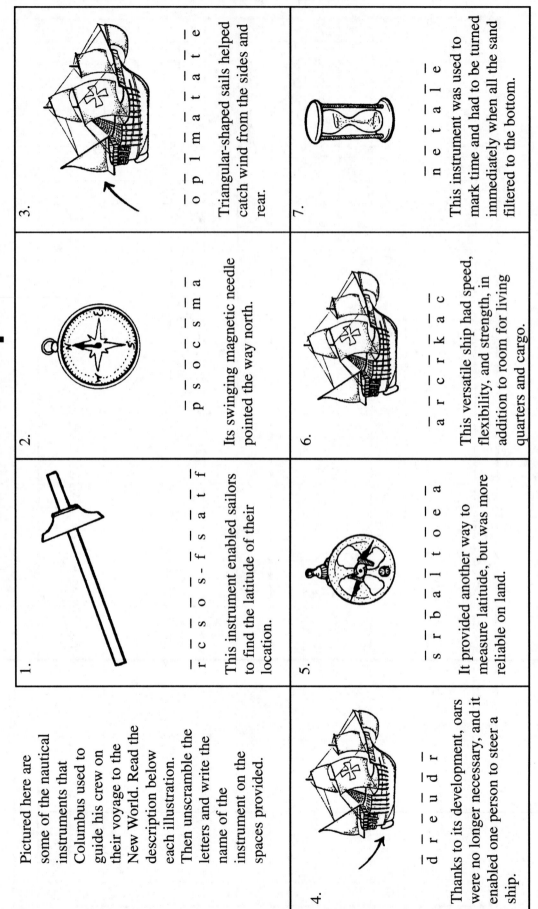

Pictured here are some of the nautical instruments that Columbus used to guide his crew on their voyage to the New World. Read the description below each illustration. Then unscramble the letters and write the name of the instrument on the spaces provided.

1.

r c s o s - f s a t f

This instrument enabled sailors to find the latitude of their location.

2.

p s o c s m a

Its swinging magnetic needle pointed the way north.

3.

o p l m a t a t e

Triangular-shaped sails helped catch wind from the sides and rear.

4.

d r e u d r

Thanks to its development, oars were no longer necessary, and it enabled one person to steer a ship.

5.

s r b a l t o e a

It provided another way to measure latitude, but was more reliable on land.

6.

a r c r k a c

This versatile ship had speed, flexibility, and strength, in addition to room for living quarters and cargo.

7.

n e t a l e

This instrument was used to mark time and had to be turned immediately when all the sand filtered to the bottom.

WORD BANK

rudder   lateen   ampoletta   astrolabe   cross-staff   carrack   compass

Know the Facts

Test your knowledge of the facts found in *The Log of Christopher Columbus. . .* by writing the answer that fits each description below. Use the Word Bank to help you.

1. city and country from which Columbus sailed	
2. measure of nautical miles	
3. the Admiral	
4. reward for first spotting land	
5. Rabihorcado	
6. island where volcano was spotted	
7. Captain of the *Pinta*	
8. these fish flew onto the deck	
9. the swiftest of the three ships	
10. another name for dolphins	
11. native canoes were made from these	
12. gifts Columbus gave the natives	
13. one of the first birds spotted at sea	
14. crustacean found among the river weeds	
15. gifts the natives gave to the crewmen	

Word Bank

10,000 maradevis	flying fish	Palos, Spain	parrots	man-of-war bird
Martin Alonzo Pinzon	red caps	tree trunks	*Pinta*	tern
Christopher Columbus	Teneriffe	dories	crab	league

Match Up

Evaluate students' listening skills and word knowledge by playing this match-up game. First, copy the fifteen words in the box below onto a chalkboard or overhead projector for all to see, or give each student a copy of the Word Box. Then tell the students to write their name at the top of a sheet of paper and number it from 1 to 15. When everyone is ready, read the first definition. Repeat it only once and allow students enough time to find and write the correct answer. Continue in this manner until all words have been defined. Direct the students to exchange papers for correction. Re-read each definition and discuss with students the correct response after each one.

Word Box

stationary	currents	disgorge	alter	league
reckoned	provisions	caravels	tranquil	prominent
lateen	feigned	linger	temperate	vessel

1. Another name for sailing ship *(vessel)*

2. These triangular sails enabled ships to sail into the wind *(lateen)*

3. Supplies such as food, water, and meat *(provisions)*

4. Ships which had lateen sails *(caravels)*

5. A measure of distance, approximately three miles *(league)*

6. Another word for counted, e.g. sixty leagues were *(reckoned)*

7. The flow of water in a general direction *(currents)*

8. Moderate or mild *(temperate)*

9. To remain still or to stay in one place *(stationary)*

10. Pretended or lied about *(feigned)*

11. To change plans or a course *(alter)*

12. Stuck out; the natives' bellies were not *(prominent)*

13. Continue to stay; to loiter *(linger)*

14. Spit up or empty the contents of the stomach *(disgorge)*

15. Peaceful and calm with no movement *(tranquil)*

Extensions:

- Pair the students. Have them find each word from the Word Box above in the text of *The Log of Christopher Columbus.* . . . Tell them to copy the sentence in which each word appears.

- Have individuals or pairs prepare a crossword puzzle using at least ten of the words from the Word Box.

- Tell the students to write a story using as many of the words from the Word Box as they can.

Columbus' Route

Label the following on the map below: Palos, Spain; Canary Islands; Cape Verde Islands; Africa; Azores Islands; and the Bahama Islands. Then draw a line to show the route and stops along Columbus' journey. Write the date at the site of each stop along the way; include the date at the very beginning of the voyage.

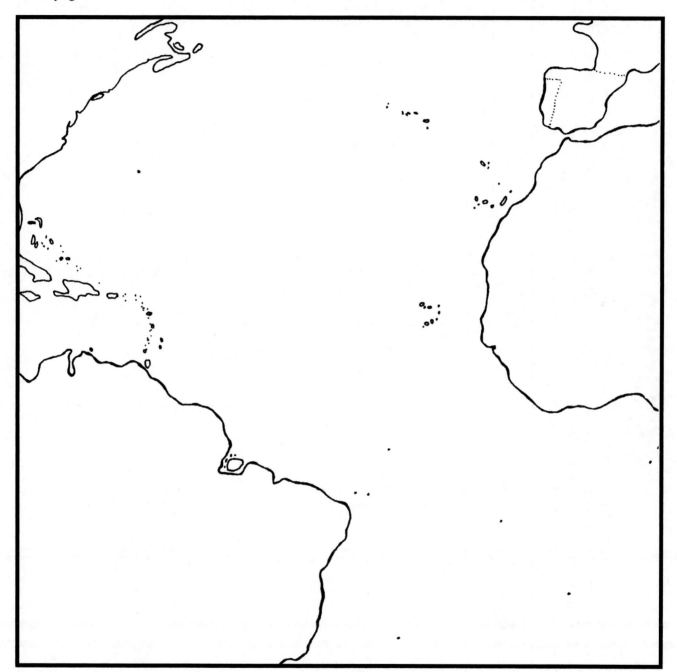

Extension:

On a map or globe measure the actual distance traveled by Columbus' fleet. Find out how long the same journey would take on a modern ocean liner.

The Green Cross

When the three ships arrived at Guanahani, Columbus and a chosen group of soldiers went ashore. The two captains each carried a banner of the Green Cross. This banner "...contained the initials of the King and Queen on each side of the cross, and a crown over each letter." Draw and color a picture of the Green Cross in the left space below. In the right space, draw and color a picture of a flag that your country might use if they were to explore a new uncharted land today. Write a name for your flag on the line provided.

The Green Cross

Comprehension Game

Test and enhance student comprehension with this easy idea. First, divide the students into groups and further divide each group into competing halves. Next, make enough copies of the task strips, below, so that each group has a complete set. Then cut apart the task strips for each group; place the strips in a small paper sack. After determining which half in each group plays first, that half draws a strip and answers the question. If they answer correctly, they score one point for their team. If they cannot answer the question, but the other team can, that team scores two points. It is then the second team's turn to draw a question. After all questions have been answered, add up the points to determine the winner. **Note:** Direct the students to record their answers on a sheet of paper. Review the questions orally as a whole class and have students check their written responses.

1. Name two examples of evidence that land could be reached by traveling west.	15. What was Columbus' purpose in taking six natives back to Spain?
2. Explain why Gomez Rascon and Christopher Quintero tampered with the *Pinta*'s rudder.	16. Why did Columbus forbid his men to take cotton from the natives?
3. Explain why Columbus underreported the number of leagues sailed each day.	17. Why did Columbus keep a log of the voyage?
4. Tell why the men were so pleased to find weeds and a river crab floating in the water.	18. What were the ". . . great flames of fire . . ." seen on the island of Teneriffe?
5. Name two purposes Columbus had for sailing to the West.	19. What is a lateen sail?
6. Explain why the sailors would become upset when they were in calm water.	20. What was the ". . . marvelous bolt of fire. . ." that fell from the sky?
7. Two reckonings were kept of the number of leagues sailed daily. Why?	21. Tell what the men thought the " . . . mass of dark, heavy clouds . . ." signaled.
8. What was the crew's method of bathing?	22. Why did the men think the sighting of the whale meant land was near?
9. Little progress was made when the wind was calm. Why?	23. Explain " . . . in these seas no wind ever blew in the direction of Spain."
10. Explain why the three vessels tried to outsail one another.	24. Tell how the man-of-war bird or Rabihorcado gets its food.
11. What method did the Portuguese use to discover most of the islands they possessed?	25. Explain why Columbus thought the Native Americans had no weapons.
12. How did Columbus encourage the men to go on with their long voyage?	26. How did Columbus and the natives communicate with each other?
13. Why did Columbus offer trinkets to the natives?	27. In what way were the natives like the Canarians?
14. Explain why Columbus believed the natives to be a poor people.	28. Why did Columbus believe the Indians " . . .would readily become Christians . . ."?

Character Traits

As with any person, Columbus had both strong and weak character traits. For example, he was respectful of King Ferdinand and Queen Isabella; in his letter to them, Columbus details how he will carry out their orders. On the other hand, Columbus was disrespectful of the natives, as he considered them to make good servants. He even took six of them back to Spain with him. These traits or characteristics are demonstrated through events in *The Log of Christopher Columbus' First Voyage to America*. Below are some other traits that made Columbus who he was. Write the event from the bottom of the page that demonstrates each trait in the proper rectangular box.

Demanding	Stubborn	Adventurous

Untruthful	*Christopher Columbus*	Thorough

Observant	Confident	Encouraging

Events:

- He felt sure that the spot of light he'd seen moving up and down signaled land.
- Columbus kept a detailed log of sights, events, and measurements.
- The men would be scolded for steering even half a point off course.
- Columbus dared to sail unknown waters.
- When the men complained, Columbus reminded them of the advantages they might gain from the trip.
- He took the appearance of birds, whales, and seaweed as evidence of land.
- Columbus refused to turn back despite the men's pleas.
- Fewer leagues were recorded than were actually traveled.

Challenge:

Think of one more character trait which describes Columbus and tell which event demonstrates that trait. Write the trait and event on the back of this page.

Write About It

The creative writing ideas below can be used in a number of ways.

1. Write a different one each day on the chalkboard. Have the students record it in a journal and write for 15 minutes (or any other specified amount of time) on the topic.

2. Cut apart the strips. Glue to tagboard and laminate for extra durability, if desired. Store the strips in a manila envelope at the classroom Creative Writing Center. Students may work on the project of their choice or you may assign all the topics to be completed within a specified time limit. (**Note:** To simplify record-keeping, attach a copy of the Quick Check, page 71, to the front of the envelope. Have the students chart their progress on this form.)

3. Pair or group the students. Place the cut-apart task cards in a bag or box. Allow each pair or group to choose a card for their assignment.

---

1. On Saturday, September 1, 1492, the crew "saw great flames of fire burst from a high mountain on the island of Teneriffe." You are a crew member. Write in your journal what you think this phenomena might be. Tell if it scared you. Describe the sights, sounds, and smells. Draw and color a picture illustrating your words.

---

2. By Wednesday, October 10, 1492, the crew voiced their concern about the length of the voyage. Imagine you were Columbus. Write a speech that you would deliver to your men. Remember, they are scared and are sailing in uncharted waters. What will you say to calm their fears?

---

3. Columbus and his men were very surprised at the appearance of the natives. Write a letter home describing these people. Include ways in which they were like people in your home town and ways in which they were different than any of the people you have ever seen.

---

4. Some of Columbus' men exchanged possessions with the natives who first offered balls of cotton, parrots, and javelins to the sailors. If you were one of Columbus' crewmen, which one of the three objects would your rather have? Explain why. Tell what you would offer in return.

---

5. Since you have been at sea you have seen many unusual sights—seaweed, crabs, sandpipers, dolphins, man-of-war birds, and even a whale. Explain the significance of these sightings to the peace of mind of the crew. Which sighting do you think proved the most comforting to the crew?

---

6. You are the official news reporter for the King and Queen. You have been allowed to accompany Columbus on his voyage so that you may record history in the making. Write a news report about Columbus' momentous meeting with the natives on Guanahani. (For more information about news reports, see page 28.)

Write About It *(cont.)*

7. Land has finally been spotted. In the darkness there is too much chance of running into rocks, so the ships are ordered to drop anchor and wait for daylight. What thoughts are going through your mind? Will you and your shipmates be able to sleep? What will you be saying to one another? Write a conversation you might have with a shipmate.

8. Explorers were searching for a direct, safe sea route to the east. The Portuguese thought they should circumnavigate Africa. However, they didn't know the exact size or shape of Africa. Some were afraid they would burn to death at the equator's "fiery waters." Write about a fear you might have if you were an explorer in the late 1400's.

9. Gromets or the ship's boys took turns watching the half-hour sand glass. As soon as the sand filtered to the bottom they turned the ampoletta over. Then they loudly sang a song to announce the ending of another half hour. Compose the words to a song or a poem about your apprehension about sailing into uncharted waters.

10. Columbus and his men were devoted Christians. In the morning, the crew would gather together to recite prayers, and in the evening they would all sing a hymn of praise to Mary, the Queen of Heaven. Write a prayer that you might have recited if you were one of the crew. Keep in mind that you are apprehensive about sailing into uncharted waters.

11. You and your crew mates have been sailing for days in uncharted waters. No land has been sighted, despite plenty of signs. Sometimes there is no wind—a very bad sign. Sometimes the compass needle does not point north as it is supposed to. You and many of the others want to turn back. Write about a plan you have to overthrow Columbus.

12. Pretend that you are a native. One morning you wake up and see strange looking boats in the water. Even stranger are the men who are emerging from the boats onto shore. They have white skin and their bodies are covered with material. Did they come from heaven? As a native, write an explanation for the foreigners' sudden appearance.

13. Columbus had brought an interpreter who spoke Arabic. He expected that to be the language spoken by the Native Americans. Unfortunately, that was not the case. Both Columbus and the Native Americans began to use hand gestures for communication. Write a dictionary of helpful hand gestures and their meanings. Draw a picture for each word.

14. During the exploration of the islands you have been treated to some of the local products including kidney beans, sweet potatoes, and maize (corn). You enjoy these foods and would like some for your friends and family, but the natives cannot spare any of these items. How would you describe them to those back home?

15. Columbus explored the other islands until Christmas. After the new year in 1493, the return voyage was begun. When they ran into fierce storms, Columbus worried they would not return to Spain safely. He wanted his story told so he wrote on parchment, wrapped it in wax cloth, sealed it in a barrel, and threw it out to sea. Write your own story as if you were Columbus.

Math on Board

Work with a partner to figure out the answers to the math problems below. All are based on figures and information found in *The Log of Christopher Columbus. . . .*

I. Record the actual number of leagues sailed on each date listed below. Then answer the questions. Friday, August 3, 1492 _____ Sunday, August 5, 1492 _____

Monday, August 6, 1492 _____ Tuesday, August 7, 1492 _____

1. On which day did they sail the most leagues? _____

2. On which day did they sail the least leagues? _____

3. During those four days how many leagues were sailed in total? _____

4. Find the average number of leagues sailed per day. _____

5. On which day was the average number of leagues sailed? _____

II. Read the information given and answer the questions.

On Friday, October 5, 1492, the crew sailed 57 leagues day and night; 45 leagues was the reckoning given to the crew.

1. What was the average number of actual leagues sailed per hour on that Friday? _____

2. At that rate, how far would they sail in six hours?_____

3. What is the difference between the actual distance sailed and the reckoning given to the crew?

   _____

III. After reading the paragraph below, answer the questions that follow.

On Monday October 1, 1492, the Admiral's pilot determined that Hierro was 578 leagues to the West. It was reported to the crew as 584 leagues, but the actual distance was 707 leagues.

1. What is the difference between the number of leagues reported to the crew and the actual distance?

   _____

2. What information in the above paragraph was not needed to solve the problem in number one?

   _____

IV. Columbus and his crew left Palos, Spain, on Friday, August 3, 1492; they arrived at an island on

Friday, October 12, 1492. How many days was that? _____

How many hours is that?_____

More Math on Board

These math problems contain some very interesting facts about Columbus. See what you can learn when you solve the following problems.

1. On Columbus' first voyage, he commanded a fleet of three ships, the *Niña*, the *Pinta*, and the *Santa María*. The ships were quite small; they carried few men aboard on that initial journey. Forty men were on the *Santa María*, 24 on the *Niña*, and 26 on the *Pinta*. How many crewman were there altogether? _____

2. If each crewman aboard the three ships was allowed two loaves of bread per day, how many loaves would be needed for a three day trip? _____

3. King Ferdinand and Queen Isabella offered 10,000 maradevis per year for life to the man who first spotted land. If one maradevi is worth one cent in gold, how many dollars in gold are 10,000 maradevis worth?_____

4. If the first man to see land on the voyage lived for ten more years, how many dollars in gold would he receive altogether? _____

5. A sailor's wages were 1,000 maradevis per month. How many dollars in gold is that? _____

6. Columbus determined the earth's circumference to be 20,000 miles. The actual distance is 25,000 miles. What is the difference between the actual and Columbus' measurement? _____

7. A sea league is 2.82 nautical miles. If the fleet sailed 59 leagues in one 24-hour period, how many nautical miles did they sail?_____

8. Columbus was born in Genoa, Italy, in the year 1451. He died in 1506. How old was he when he died? _____

9. Columbus lived in Lisbon, Portugal, from 1476 to 1485. How many years did he live in Portugal? _____

10. During Columbus' last voyage—the High Voyage—only 116 men were left after deaths and desertions. One hundred forty men began the voyage. How many died or deserted? _____

Common Constellations

Early navigators relied on the stars to help them chart their course. Below are some of the more commonly known and easily viewed constellations. Read and learn about these star clusters. Try to find them in the night sky, or use them to help you make your own planetarium (see page 26).

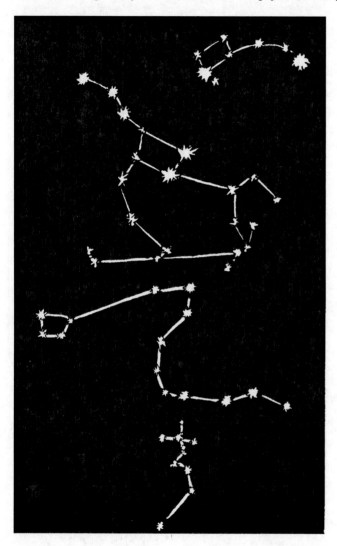

Little Dipper or Ursa Minor

The first star in the handle of the Little Dipper is the North Star. This star always points north. The Little Dipper can be seen in the northern sky all year long.

Big Dipper or Ursa Major

Use the Big Dipper to help find the North Star. Imagine a line through the two outside stars of the cup. Keep looking up until the North Star is visible. Columbus knew that the North Star held its place in the sky while all the others star groups kept moving.

Draco or The Dragon

According to Greek legend, Ladon the sleeping dragon was told to guard Hera's apple tree. One day Heracles tricked Ladon and sliced off his head. To punish Ladon, Hera changed him into a constellation of stars—Draco, the Dragon.

Casseopeia or The Queen

Casseopeia was a boastful queen who often bragged about her own and her daughter's beauty. The gods punished her by making her appear upside down. Thus, depending on the season Casseopeia looks like a W or an M.

On Your Own Projects

- The Ancient Greeks used mythology to explain the various constellations. Research and write a report about how one of the constellations got its name. An excellent resource book for this project is *The Stargazer's Guide to the Galaxy* by Q.L. Pearce (RGA Publishing Group, 1991).

- In our sky there are 88 constellations. Find out and list all 88 names.

- Find out your astrological sign. Draw a picture of your sign's constellation.

- Read and learn the definition of "star."

- Draw the stars in the constellation of your choice. Then draw the figure it represents. For example, if you have chosen Casseopeia, draw the W arrangement of stars and then the Queen.

- What does Ursa in Ursa Major and Ursa Minor refer to?

Meteors and Comets

During Columbus' first voyage to the Indies he reported seeing "...a marvelous bolt of fire fall from the heavens into the sea..." This phenomenon was actually a meteor. Learn about meteors. Read the paragraph below and then answer the questions below it.

Meteors are sometimes called "shooting stars," but they are not stars at all. They are chunks of iron and stone that have broken off from asteroids. Meteors fall to Earth very quickly and, unlike comets, they only appear to last for a few seconds. As meteors make their descent, they become hot and begin to glow brightly. Meteors can burn up before they reach the Earth, but occasionally a meteor will hit the ground hard enough to form a crater. When a meteor makes it all the way to Earth, it is then called a meteorite. One famous meteor crater is in Arizona. The Barringer Meteor Crater is almost 600 feet deep and was made by a giant meteorite weighing more than 500 tons (or one million pounds)!

Other bright objects which can be seen traveling through space are comets. A comet is a ball of dust, ice, and gases that travels in an orbit around the sun. As it speeds along in space, the sun's light and heat cause the comet to lose some of its dust and gas. This dust and gas streams out from behind the comet forming a tail millions of miles long. Probably the most famous comet is Halley's comet, named after English astronomer Edmund Halley. He observed and studied the comet in 1682; he predicted that it would reappear in 1759. Halley's comet has been seen every 76 years since the year 240 B.C. It was last seen in 1986. In what year will the next sighting take place?

Read each statement below. Write a **T** if the sentence is true; write an **F** if the sentence is false.

1. _____ All meteors burn up before they reach the earth.

2. _____ A comet orbits the earth.

3. _____ Meteors are composed of iron and stone.

4. _____ As meteors fall to the ground they cool off.

5. _____ The Barringer Meteor Crater can be found in Arizona.

6. _____ Comets are the same as meteors.

7. _____ Meteors are stars.

8. _____ Another name for meteor is "shooting star."

9. _____ Halley's Comet will be seen in 1999.

10. _____ Some meteors hit the ground hard enough to form craters.

11. _____ A comet has a tail millions of miles long.

12. _____ Meteors glow brightly as they make their descent.

Challenge: Complete a Venn diagram (page 63) comparing meteors and comets.

22

Latitude and Longitude

Read the paragraphs below. Then find and label the boldfaced words on the globe.

> Maps and globes utilize a system of intersecting lines to find exact locations of places on Earth. All of these lines are built from the **North Pole**, the **South Pole**, and the **Equator**.
>
> ***Lines of latitude*** are parallel to one another; they tell the distance north or south in degrees (°). Since the equator is exactly in the middle, its latitude is zero degrees (0°).
>
> ***Lines of longitude*** or meridians, tell how far east or west. These vertical lines extend from the North Pole to the South Pole. The longitude east or west is measured in degrees from the ***prime meridian*** (also known as the Greenwich meridian).

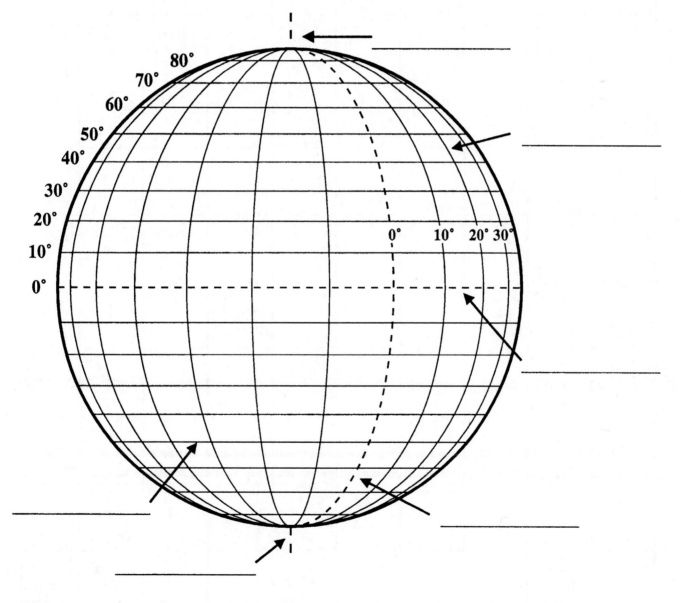

Challenge: Find these on an actual globe.

Voyage to the Indies Game

Cut out the game board below and glue to the inside of a file folder. Directions continue on the next page.

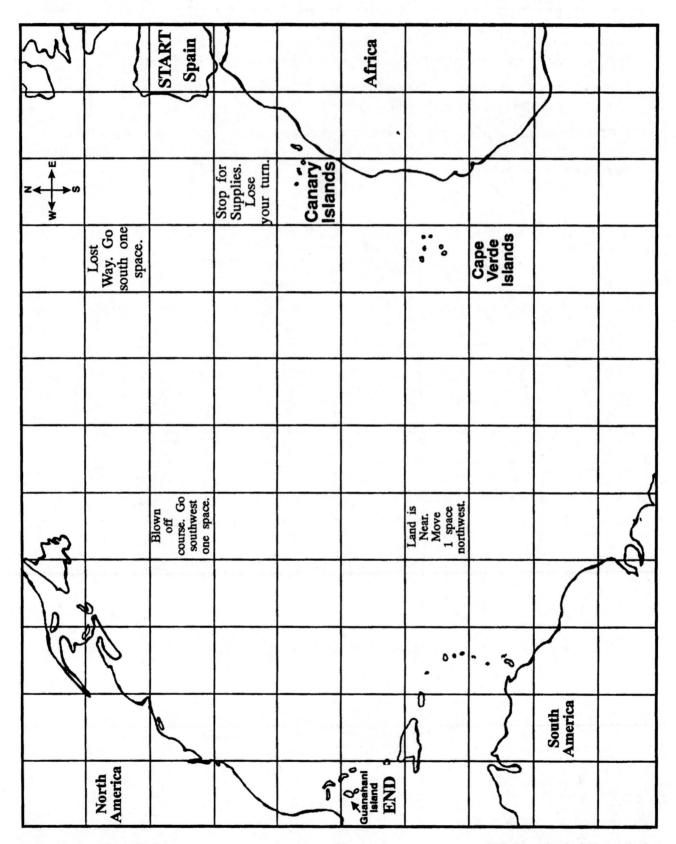

Voyage to the Indies Game *(cont.)*

How to Play

- Two to four may play. Each will need a marker (buttons, coins, beans, etc.).

- Shuffle the game cards and place them face down in a pile.

- All players begin at Spain. In turn, players take a Game Card (see below) and read its directions. Each player may choose to follow the directions on the card, or remain in the same spot until the next turn. Used game cards are to be placed in a separate pile to be shuffled and reused when the original pile is depleted. If a player can't move as directed, the card is placed in the used pile and a new card is drawn.

- The first player to reach Guanahani wins.

Game Cards

Cut apart and store in an envelope attached to the back of the file folder.

Move 1 space **EAST**	Move 2 spaces **SOUTH**	Move 1 space **WEST**	Move 2 spaces **SOUTHWEST**
Move 1 space **EAST**	Move 2 spaces **SOUTH**	Move 1 space **WEST**	Move 2 spaces **SOUTHWEST**
Move 2 spaces **EAST**	Move 1 space **WEST**	Move 1 space **WEST**	Move 1 space **NORTHEAST**
Move 1 space **NORTH**	Move 1 space **WEST**	Move 2 spaces **WEST**	Move 1 space **NORTHEAST**
Move 1 space **NORTH**	Move 1 space **WEST**	Move 2 spaces **WEST**	Move 1 space **NORTHEAST**
Move 1 space **SOUTH**	Move 1 space **WEST**	Move 1 space **SOUTHWEST**	Move 1 space **NORTHEAST**
Move 1 space **SOUTH**	Move 1 space **WEST**	Move 1 space **SOUTHWEST**	**ONE FREE MOVE in any direction of your choice**

Science Projects

The science projects below are quick, fun, and require minimal preparation. Pair or group the students if desired, but these ideas may also be completed individually or demonstrated to the whole class by an instructor.

Planetarium in a Box

Materials: cereal box; pencil; flashlight

Directions:

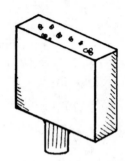

- With the pencil, punch a pattern of stars in the unopened end of the cereal box. (For some star patterns see page 21).
- Darken the room. Shine a flashlight up through the box towards the ceiling.

Dish Compass

Materials: one large sewing needle; piece of cork or foam packaging material; saucer; water; magnet

Directions:

- Partially fill the saucer with water.
- Slide one end of the magnet along the length of the needle in the same direction 20 times. (This process is called magnetizing and will turn the needle into a magnet.)

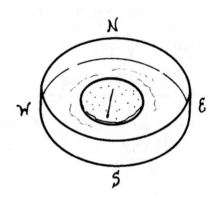

- Place the newly magnetized needle on the cork or foam and float it on the water in the saucer.
- Watch as the needle settles into a north–south pattern.

Miniature Volcano

Materials: baking powder; vinegar; red food coloring; plastic bottle cap (from soft drink bottles or food containers); teaspoon; soda straw

Directions:

- Fill the bottle cap with baking powder.
- Cover the baking powder with two or three drops of red food coloring.
- With a soda straw, slowly drip about a teaspoon of vinegar onto the baking powder; red lava will foam down the sides of the bottle cap volcano.

Variation: To make a volcano more realistic, mold clay or dough (see recipe below) into the shape of a volcano. Allow to dry. Proceed with the instructions above.

Dough Recipe

In a bowl, mix one cup each of flour, salt, and water. Knead until dough is smooth. Shape into a volcano; with the thumb, make an indentation at the top or insert a bottle cap. Allow to dry. Proceed as above.

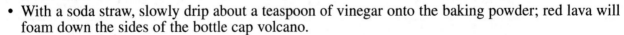

Artworks

Some suitable art subjects to complement your studies of Columbus are outlined below. They can be used at anytime during the unit or as part of a culminating activity.

Volcanic Art

Materials: black or other dark construction paper; liquid bleach; cotton swabs; straws; spoons
Directions:

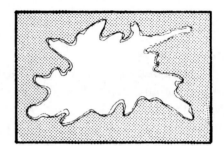

- Pour liquid bleach into a cup.

- Spoon some bleach onto a sheet of construction paper.

- Immediately spread the bleach with the spoon or blow through the straw to move the bleach on the paper.

- Try painting with a swab dipped in bleach, if desired, or after applying bleach on the paper, tilt in many direction.

- Dry and display on the walls.

Native American Masks

Materials: paper plates, paper bags, or cereal boxes; scissors; string or yarn; pipe cleaners, construction paper, glue, markers, poster paints, and other decorative items

Directions:

- Decorate the plates with black, red, or white paint. Cut out holes for eyes. Attach a length of yarn to each side of the mask.

- Cut off the back of the cereal box; cover with construction paper. Cut out eyes and nose; with chalk draw mouth, hair, and painted designs. Attach a length of yarn to each side of the mask.

- Make sure the bag is large enough to fit over the head. Cut out eyes, nose, and mouth. Paint designs on the face. Attach yarn hair to the top of the bag mask.

Star Tracks

Materials: black and white construction paper; glue; one-hole punch; pencil; scissors

Directions:

- Cut one sheet of black and one sheet of white construction paper to a 5" x 7" size.

- With a pencil, lightly draw the outline of an original constellation or an actual pattern (see page 21 for some samples) on a 5" x 7" sheet of white construction paper.

- Use the paper punch to cut out holes from one 5" x 7" sheet of black construction paper.

- Glue the punched out circles to the outline of the constellation drawn on the white sheet of paper.

- As a variation, punch holes in white construction paper and glue to black construction paper.

The Snake

- Have the students write titles for their creations.

The 5 W's and How

A well-written newspaper article contains what are known as the Five W's (who, what, when, where, why) and HOW. Each of these elements should be present so that the reader has a clear understanding of the news. Reporters use the Five W's and HOW to organize the information and to make sure that all the important facts are included in an article or story.

Read each article below. On the lines provided write the who, what, when, where, why, and how of each story. Use the information at the bottom of this page to help you determine them.

On Friday, August 3, 1492, at 8 a.m. Christopher Columbus set sail from Palos, Spain. He commanded a fleet of three ships— the *Niña*, the *Pinta*, and the *Santa María*. Columbus expects to find a new route to the Indies by sailing west, instead of east.

Who: _____
What: _____
When: _____
Where: _____
Why: _____
How: _____

Captain Martin Alonzo Pinzon reported that the *Pinta*'s rudder had broken loose just three days into the journey. The mishap occurred close enough to the Canary Islands that the crew could stop and repair the ship. Two sailors were blamed for sabotaging the ship because both men had expressed their fears about going on such a long voyage.

Who: _____
What: _____
When: _____
Where: _____
Why: _____
How: _____

After several indications that land was near, Admiral Columbus sighted it at two o'clock in the morning on Friday, October 12, 1492. He was high on the castle of the poop deck when he spotted a light moving up and down. Because of the darkness, the Admiral ordered the ship to shorten sail and wait for daylight.

Who: _____
What: _____
When: _____
Where: _____
Why: _____
How: _____

Your Turn: Write your own article about Columbus. Be sure to include the 5 W's and How.

Five W's and HOW

1. **Who** is it about?
2. **What** happened?
3. **When** did it happen?
4. **Where** did it happen?
5. **Why** did it happen?
6. **How** did it happen?

An Explorer's Picnic

Culminate your study of Columbus with an explorer's picnic. Students can experience life on board a small ship, eat sea rations, and play a game of Shipwrecked. They can also write letters home or write entries in their diaries. Directions for these activities appear below and on the next page.

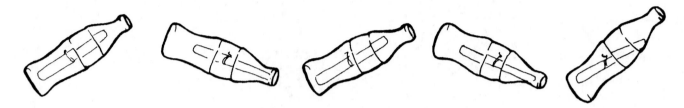

Life on Board

Columbus' Flagship, the *Santa Maria*, was approximately 78 feet long. With string or yarn have the students measure a 78-foot long line on the playground, gym, or other unobstructed area. This can be accomplished by assigning twenty-six students to measure a yard of string or yarn. The other students can be responsible for taping the ends of the string or yarn together. Gently stretch out the length of yarn or string. Draw an oval 12 feet at its widest with chalk (if measuring on pavement) or make a masking tape border if working on a floor surface. Tell the students to get on board but they may not move outside of the boundaries. No books, toys, or any other objects will be allowed on board. Have the students imagine what it would be like to sail for endless days with no land in sight and nothing to amuse them. Direct them to write about their feelings and experiences in a letter home or in a journal.

Letters in a Bottle

Use the bottle form on the top of page 30 to have students write a letter explaining how it feels to be at sea so far from land, or describing the wondrous sights they have seen on their voyage. Roll the letters to fit through the neck of a clean, empty soda bottle. (Rubber bands around the letters make removal easier.) Seal the bottle with its lid and "float" it to another classroom for reading and response.

Journals

Use the form on the bottom of page 30 for students to write journal entries similar to those written by Columbus. To compile all entries into a class book, simply punch two holes along the left sides, stack, thread a length of yarn or string through the holes, and tie with a bow. Add the journal to the classroom library.

Sea Rations

Serve this menu which is based on the actual foods that were stored on board the vessels: beef jerky, cheese, raisins, biscuits and honey, and water.

Shipwrecked

Arrange six old tires in the playing area. Each tire is an island where a player is "safe." Two players are chosen to be "it"; both of them try to tag the other players. Once tagged, that person joins those who are "it." Players may jump into an island to be "safe," but must return to play after ten seconds. (Have them count slowly to ten.) Note: Old towels or small rugs may be used if tires are unavailable.

The Log of Christopher Columbus' First Voyage to America

Use with activities on page 29.

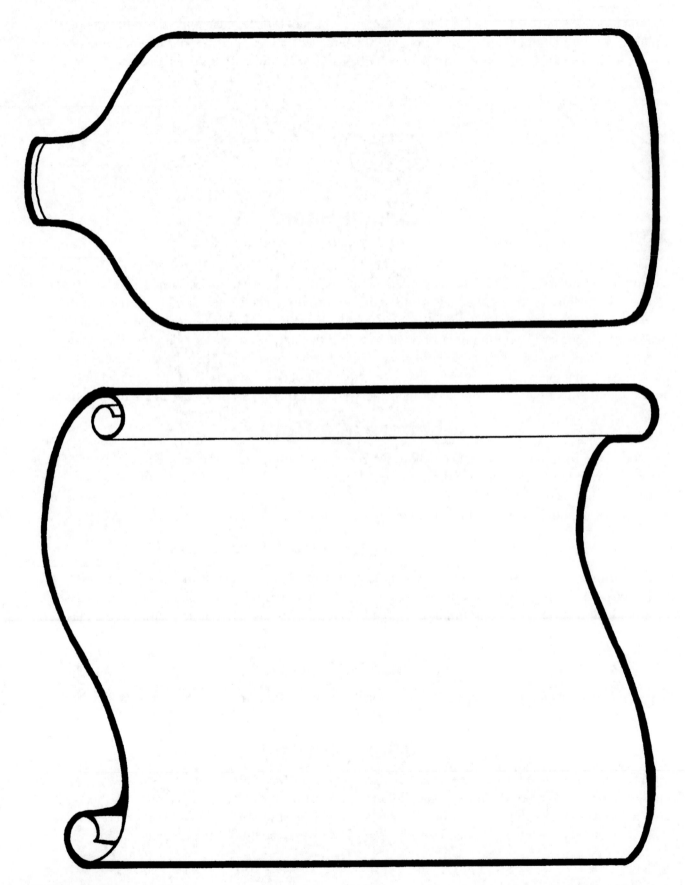

The Usborne Book of Explorers

by Felicity Everett and Struan Reid

Summary

The Usborne Book of Explorers *contains the history of exploration from the beginning of people to the present. Instead of presenting the information chronologically, however, the text is arranged into geographical regions including Africa, Asia, the Americas, and Australia. Individual pages cover an assortment of other topics which include Arabia, the Poles, Circumnavigation, Mountains, Undersea, and Space. Accompanying each section is a map of that particular area and a chart of the most important dates in that region's exploration. The two final pages in this book contain a master list of the key dates in world exploration.*

All of these features make *The Usborne Book of Explorers* a great introduction to the subject of explorers and exploration. As you complete the activities on pages 31 to 56 determine which topics the students are most interested in. Plan more detailed lessons based on their interests.

Sample Plan

Day I

- Display an Explorer's Bulletin Board. (pages 73 to 76)
- Put explorations in chronological order on Time Line. (page 35)
- Construct an Explorer's Web; save for future reference.
- Research. Student pairs can complete Explorer Report. (page 36)

Day II

- Begin reading; divide it into manageable segments with Through the Pages. (37 to 40)
- Students make review cards. (#2, page 32)
- Assess student knowledge with Explorer Review on page 41.
- Do whole group vocabulary chalkboard activity, It's All in the Name. (page 42)

Day III

- Expand Vocabulary. Choose from the strategies listed with the Exploration Word Bank. (page 43)
- Categorizing: Three of a Kind. (page 47)
- Reading. Impact. (page 45)
- Math. Review basic math skills with Voyage Math. (page 50)

Day IV

- Critical Thinking Skills: Cause and Effect. (page 46)
- Compare and contrast. (page 44)
- Creative Writing Topics (page 48)

Day V

- Conduct a Math Lab. (page 49)
- Explorers' Riches. (page 51)
- Research and Critical Thinking. Spanish and Aztec Armor (page 52)
- Art. Choose from three projects on page 53

Day VI

- Make Coat of Arms Big Books. (page 54)
- Culminating Activity: Spicy Affair. (pages 55 and 56)
- Suggestions for further reading. (page 34)
- Learn about Women Explorers (page 34)

Overview of Activities

SETTING THE STAGE

1. **Set the mood with an Explorers' Bulletin Board** (see page 73 to 76 for patterns and directions). Add to it as the unit progresses.

2. **Explorers Time Line.** Have on hand a supply of atlases, history books, biographies, and other books about explorers. Divide the students into small groups. Give each group an Explorer's Time Line worksheet (page 35) to complete. Encourage them to use as many of the reference books as they need.

3. **Create a web about explorers.** Brainstorm definitions, names of explorers, types of exploration, and other related topics. Save and add to it throughout the unit. Use it as a means to review what was learned and as an idea bank for writing stories or reports.

4. **Research Explorers.** In *The Usborne Book of Explorers* the stories of almost 50 different men are highlighted. Assign each pair or small group of students a different explorer to research. Have them write an Explorer Report. (See page 36.) Use a three hole punch on the completed pages and compile them into a loose-leaf binder. Add it to the classroom library.

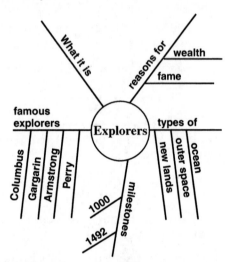

ENJOYING THE BOOK

1. **Through the Pages.** Before reading a section of text assign students the section-specific activities so they know what information to look for. A different strategy to use rather than reading the text page-by-page is to assign each group of students a different continent. Have them read those pages which pertain to their assigned area. Follow-up with the section-specific activities on pages 37 to 40.

2. **Fact Cards.** As the students read each segment, have them write one important fact they learned from the material. Tell them to write their fact on a small index card. Hole punch the cards and add them to a ring. Student pairs can use the cards to review material. Later, develop test questions based on the facts gathered.

3. **Assessment.** Assess students' knowledge of the various explorers with the Explorer Review lesson presented on page 41. At the end of the unit you may want to administer this test again to assess student progress.

4. **It's All in the Name.** Reinforce the vocabulary of the text with the chalkboard activity outlined on page 42. You may want to make a transparency of the page.

5. **Word Knowledge.** Develop and expand vocabulary with any of the ideas outlined on the Exploration Word Bank, page 43. Some words are given to help you get started but you may want to add your own words to the list.

Overview of Activities *(cont.)*

ENYOYING THE BOOK *(cont.)*

6. **Compare and Contrast.** Before assigning the activity on page 44 you may want to model the process with students. Draw a simple chart on the chalkboard (see example at right). Brainstorm with students some facts they know about the two men. Determine which section each statement would fit into most appropriately before recording it. Any two explorers may be compared but it will be easier if students are quite familiar with the two.

Columbus	discovered a new world felt he was unappreciated
Both	were explorers sailed for Spain
Magellan	first to sail around world killed by natives

7. **Reading.** As students read the story on the Impact worksheet (page 45), they must unscramble letters to make words that will complete each sentence. With the whole group, review and reread the paragraphs.

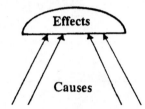

8. **Cause and Effect.** Develop critical thinking skills with the technique outlined on page 46. The shape can be changed to suit your own tastes. More important is the procedure. Step-by-step directions are provided. Some sample topics and their causes are also given.

9. **Critical Thinking.** Sharpen students' categorizing skills with the lesson presented on page 47. Depending on your class' abilities, you may determine whether or not to supply the students with the listing of categories.

10. **Creative Writing.** Sixteen creative writing topics have been provided for you to use (see page 48). Four different ways to use the assignments have also been outlined, but you may want to design your own assignments.

11. **Math.** The text of *The Usborne Book of Explorers* offers many natural math applications. With that in mind, A Math Lab on page 49 was developed. Basic math skills for students at this level are emphasized as is practical problem solving. Conducting a math lab can best be accomplished by following the directions found on that page. If a lab is inappropriate for your class, use the problems in any way that is compatible with your teaching style.

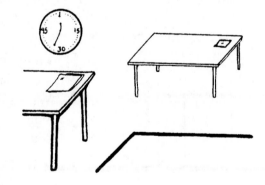

Overview of Activities *(cont.)*

ENJOYING THE BOOK *(cont.)*

12. **Voyage Math.** Page 50 is a more traditional and typical math worksheet. As students complete each problem they will learn intriguing explorer facts.

13. **Explorer's Riches** on page 51 is a fun enrichment activity that will help increase spelling, word knowledge, and thinking skills. It may be used as a regular classroom assignment, serve as extra credit, or be given for homework. Challenge students to make up their own hidden word boxes.

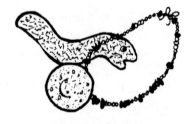

14. **Spanish and Aztec Armor.** The activity on page 52 combines research with critical thinking skills. It would be an excellent paired activity.

15. **Art.** Three unusual art activities for use during the Explorers Unit are described on page 53. Have students research Inca and Aztec artifacts before working on All that Glitters or Golden Etching.

EXTENDING THE BOOK

1. **Coat of Arms Big Book.** Three methods of making big books, and suggested big book uses for group or individual student projects are provided on page 54.

2. **A Spicy Affair.** Host a spice fair culminating activity after completing the projects outline on pages 55 and 56. Students can make glue and spice pictures, spice jewelry, and an aromatic modeling dough. They will test their olfactory senses with a sniff test and make research boards about various spices. Spiced cookies are the final treat for the fair. Invite another class to enjoy the displays and art projects with you.

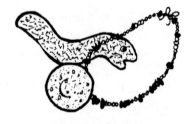

3. **Further Reading.** Encourage students to read two or more books about the same explorer. Then have them compare the versions. Were any facts different? Did any of the books downplay his faults? Which version was the most fair in presenting both sides of the story? Direct the students to create a web, Venn diagram, or chart to compare the versions. Two excellent resources to use for this activity include *Great Lives. Exploration* by Milton Lomask (Charles Scribner's Sons, 1988) and *The Great Atlas of Discovery* by Neil Grant (Dorling Kindersley, 1992).

4. **Learn About Some Women Explorers.** Although not a lot has been written about women explorers they do exist. From Sacagawea to Mary Kingsley to Sally Ride, each has made her mark in the world of exploration. Consult a librarian for materials about women explorers. Don't overlook children's magazines as a possible source of information. Students can use an Explorer Report outline (see page 36) to write about a woman explorer of their choice.

Explorers' Time Line

Work with a partner. Arrange the historical events below in correct chronological order by writing the event number on the appropriate blank.

Note: Use the index at the back of the book or other reference books to find the answers.

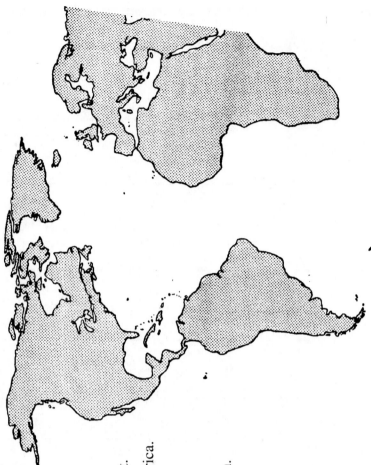

1. Vespucci explored the shores of South America.

2. Drake became the second captain to sail around the world.

3. Dias rounded the tip of South Africa into the Indian Ocean.

4. Magellan found the passage at the tip of South America.

5. Verrazano searched for a route to the Indies through the continent.

6. The Vikings founded the first European settlement in North America.

7. Hudson sailed the northern shores of Canada.

8. da Gama charted a route to India by sailing around Africa.

9. Balboa's search for gold led to the discovery of the Pacific Ocean.

10. Pizarro led a bloody battle to conquer the Incas.

11. Marco Polo and his family reached China.

12. Cortes conquered the Aztecs in Mexico.

13. A fleet of three ships led by Columbus set out to find the Indies.

14. Champlain explored the eastern shores of Canada.

1000	1275	1487	1492	1498	1500	1513	1520	1521	1523	1531	1580	1603	1610

Challenge:

Extend this time line. On a sheet of paper write the 14 events listed above in correct chronological order. Make a list of ten more events from 1610 to the present to add to the list.

Explorer Report

Explorer _____   Birth Date _____

Birth Place _____   Date of Death_____

Some Life Highlights: _____

_____

_____

_____

Best Known for: _____

_____

_____

_____

Best Qualities: _____

_____

_____

_____

Unfavorable Qualities:_____

_____

_____

_____

Resources used:

  1. Title: _____

      Author: _____   Publisher and Year: _____

  2. Title: _____

      Author: _____   Publisher and Year: _____

  3. Title: _____

      Author: _____   Publisher and Year: _____

Through the Pages

The activities presented on this and the next three pages (pages 38 to 40) are intended to be used as introductory or follow-ups to the reading on the indicated section in *The Usborne Book of Explorers*. Choose those activities which best suit your classroom needs.

Introduction

* *Pre-Reading.* On chart paper, make a class web of reasons why people explore. Save the web and add to it throughout the unit.

* *Explorers.* Talk about what qualities and characteristics a good explorer must possess. List responses. Have students decide which of the characteristics they have. Ask them if they think they would make good explorers. Tell them to defend their answers.

Ibn Battuta

* *Mapping.* Read the paragraph titled "Through the Middle East." On a map of the region or a globe have the students trace Ibn Battuta's route.

* *Dangerous Territory.* Write the following statement for all to see: *The African interior was so forbidding that after Ibn Battuta's adventure it was not explored for another 400 years.* Assign the students to find out why this region was so dangerous.

The Green Sea of Darkness

* *Caravels.* Find out more about caravels. How were they different from other sailing ships? Draw a picture of a caravel.

* *Creative Story.* Have the students read the paragraph titled "A Barrier of Fear." Pay special attention to the description of the "Green Sea of Darkness." Direct students to write a creative story and accompanying pictures about a ship which actually experienced a boiling sea, thick green fog, and monsters. Share the stories and pictures in small groups.

Searching for the River Niger and Timbuktu

* *A Novel Idea.* Explorer Rene' Caillie' was inspired by the story *Robinson Crusoe* written by Daniel Defoe. Read the novel aloud to students or assign them to read the book on their own or find out about Daniel Defoe.

* *Misadventures.* Explorer, Mungo Park, was robbed by locals, captured by horsemen, and held prisoner. For four months he was kept in an isolated hut on the edge of the desert. After returning to Scotland he wrote a book called *Travels in the Interior District of Africa.* Direct the students to write a chapter for this book.

The Source of the Nile

* *Comparisons.* After reading about Richard Burton and John Speke, make a class Venn diagram comparing these two explorers. (For a prepared comparison worksheet see page 44.)

* *Research.* Learn more about the Nile River. Assign a group of students to prepare a report about ancient life in Egypt and how the Nile contributed to all aspects of life during those times. Have the group share their findings with the rest of the class. (For additional in-depth activities about the Nile see Teacher Created Materials thematic unit *Egypt*, #292.)

Through the Pages *(cont.)*

Exploring the Heart of Africa

* *Livingstone*. Ask students all the reasons that David Livingstone traveled to Africa. Discuss each one in turn and determine if he was successful in that area or not.

* *Dear Diary*. With the class discuss the sights and sounds that might have greeted H.M. Stanley on his journey. Write a diary entry describing the rainforest, cannibals, and animals that he saw.

East Goes West

* *The Silk Road*. Divide the students into pairs or groups. Tell them to draw and label a map of China, India, and Arabia. Have them draw the route that was known as the Silk Road.

* *Junks*. Read about Chinese junks on page 15 of *The Usborne Book of Explorers*. Compare a Chinese junk with a European ship of the same time period. Listing how they were alike and different.

Marco Polo

* *Marvels*. During his travels Marco Polo enjoyed some marvelous adventures. Students can read about them in *Marco Polo. His Notebook* by Susan L. Roth (Doubleday, 1990). As an extension, have the students write a page or two to add to this book.

* *Escape*. The Khan did not want to lose his loyal servants but finally the Polo family managed to escape. Have students research this aspect of Marco's adventure writing a detailed account of how the three men got out of the country.

Vasco da Gama and the Route to India

* *Measuring the Miles*. Have students work in pairs. Give each pair a length of string and a measuring stick. Tell them to measure the number of miles da Gama traveled in his journey from Lisbon, Portugal, to Calicut, India. Make a class chart of all the pairs' measurements. Find the average for the whole class.

The Search for the Northeast Passage

* *Winter Refuge*. Dutchman Willem Barents led a crew to disaster in 1596. Their ship became stuck in ice and they had to build a hut for shelter. Have students reread the paragraph "Trapped by Ice." Direct them to draw a cutaway section of a hut they would have designed. Label all the parts they used from the ship.

The Vikings Reach America

* *Sagas*. Viking exploits were recorded in long tales called sagas. Have student groups do more research about Eric the Red or his son, Leif Ericsson, and write a saga.

* *Viking Ships*. Draw and label the parts of a Viking ship.

Christopher Columbus

* *Motto*. "Gold, God and Cathay" could be Columbus' motto. Discuss with the class the meaning of the motto. Create mottoes for Columbus or another explorer of that era.

* *A Log*. Assign students to read *The Log of Christopher Columbus' First Voyage to America* as copied by Bartholomew Las Casas (Shoe String Press, 1989) to gain insight about Columbus' true character.

Cortes

* *Armor*. Compare Spanish and Aztec armor. See page 52.

* *Conquistador*. Cortes' contact with the Aztecs resulted in the destruction of their empire. Make a class cause and effect chart of this statement.

Through the Pages *(cont.)*

The Hunt for the Northwest Passage

* *Inuits.* While searching for a Northwest passage Frobisher met some Inuits. Have students research the Inuit culture and make a list of five facts they have learned. Or, assign students to read a novel such as *Julie of the Wolves* by Jean Craighead George (Harper & Row, 1972).

The Building of New France

* *Fur and Hide.* French explorers encountered a number of different animals which they trapped for their furs and hide. Direct the students to draw a map of the area the French explored in the 1500s and early 1600s. Add pictures of elk, martens, otters, and beavers in the areas where they would most likely be found.

Across the Continent

* *Lewis and Clark.* A Native American woman guided Lewis and Clark on their expedition. Read more about her. Two excellent titles include *Stream to the River. River to the Sea: A Novel of Sacagawea* by Scott O'Dell (Houghton Mifflin, 1986) and *Sacagawea: American Pathfinder* by Flora W. Seymour (Macmillan, 1991).

* *Mileage.* Pair the students and have them measure how many miles the Lewis and Clark party traveled on their journey from St.Louis to the Pacific Ocean.

Scientists and Dreamers

* *Writing.* Have the students write an essay on the differences between explorers of the sixteenth and seventeenth centuries and explorers of the eighteenth century.

* *Word Meanings.* Charles Darwin was a naturalist, astronomer, biologist, geologist, and expert linguist. Tell students to define each term.

The Quest for a Southern Continent

* *Tahiti.* Cook's first mission was to travel to Tahiti to observe the planet Venus as it passed between the earth and the sun. Find out more about this island paradise from the book *The Remarkable Voyages of Captain Cook* by Rhoda Blumberg (Macmillan, 1991).

* *Disease.* In the eighteenth century 60% of the sailors died on long voyages. Direct the students to make a list of at least five ways in which Cook improved conditions for his sailors.

Into the Interior

* *Hardships.* Before reading this page have the students look at a map of Australia. What land features and conditions might present a problem to explorers? After reading the text discuss the actual reasons.

The Forbidden Land

* *Masterpiece.* Charles Doughty is regarded as one of the greatest explorers of Arabia and even wrote a book about his travels. Write one chapter in his book.

* *Pictures.* After reading about Johann Burckhardt's travels, have the students draw pictures of a tomb or temple he may have seen.

Around the World

* A *Chronicle.* One survivor of the Magellan exploration was a man named Pigafetta. He wrote of the poor conditions they endured and of the wondrous sights including St. Elmo's Fire. Have the students research and find out about the phenomenon known as St. Elmo's Fire.

* *Comparisons.* In a class chart, compare the voyages of Francis Drake and Ferdinand Magellan.

Through the Pages *(cont.)*

The Race for the Poles

* *First to the North Pole.* Robert Peary and Matt Henson are often credited with being the first to reach the North Pole. Learn more about the fascinating life story of Henson. Two excellent books to read are *Arctic Explorer. The Story of Matthew Henson* by Jeri Ferris (Carolrhoda Books, 1989) and *Matthew Henson* by Michael Gilman (Chelsea House, 1988).

* *A Race.* Roald Amundsen and Robert Scott were in a race to reach the South Pole first. Amundsen won for a number of reasons. As a class discuss what factors led to Amundsen's win.

The Roof of the World

* *Mapping.* Pair the students and supply each pair with a flat map of the world. Direct the students' attention to the information in the chart on page 42 of the text. Have them label the map with the ten highest mountains and the dates when they were climbed.

* *Modern Climbing.* Modern mountaineering as we know it was developed by a swiss scientist named Horace de Saussure. What innovations did he bring to mountain climbing? How does the equipment and clothing of early mountain climbers compare with that of modern climbers?

Exploring the Oceans

* *Underwater Pioneer.* Frenchman Jacques Cousteau has probably done more for underwater exploration than any other person before him. As a pioneer underwater explorer, he has written books, produced television shows, and invented a device to help with his explorations. Read more about this fascinating man in *Jacques Cousteau: Man of the Oceans* by Carol Greene (Childrens Press, 1990).

* *Videos.* Check with a video store or libraries for a copy of one of his programs; show it to the class. (His 1967 TV series was titled "The Undersea World of Jacques Cousteau.")

Beyond the Earth

* *First.* Russian Yuri Gagarin, was the first person to travel in space. In 1969, Americans Neil Armstrong and Edwin "Buzz" Aldrin became the first to walk on the moon. Direct the students to write a list of 15 different things the astronauts might have said as they explored the moon.

* *Two Endeavours.* Englishman, James Cook, was appointed lieutenant and given command of his first ship, the *Endeavour*, in 1768. Over two centuries later in 1993, another ship, named *Endeavour*, was launched in outer space to repair the orbiting Hubble telescope. With the students discuss the meaning of the word endeavour. Ask them why they think it is an appropriate name for the two ships. Compare the *Endeavour* of James Cook's era with the *Endeavour* of the twentieth century.

Extensions:

* *Research Women Explorers.* Read about river explorer Mary Kingsley in the December, 1993, issue of *Kids Discover* magazine and *Great Lives. Exploration* by Milton Lomask (Charles Scribner's Sons, 1988). Find out about some famous astronauts such as American Sally Ride and Russian Svetlana Savitskaya in *Women in Space* by Carole S. Brigg (Lerner Publications, 1988). Learn about some women on the high seas in *Seafaring Women* by Linda Orang de Pauw (Houghton Mifflin, 1988).

Explorer Review

Assess students' knowledge of explorers with this whole class activity. Direct the students to write their name at the top of a sheet of paper and number it from 1 to 12. Read aloud the clues after each number allowing enough time for students to write a response. When the quiz is complete have the students exchange papers; correct them in whole group.

Notes: *Before beginning this exercise, you may want to list the explorers' names on the chalkboard for students to choose from. *For a challenge, read only one clue for each explorer. Read the second one if you find that the class is really stumped. *Challenge the students to make up their own explorer clues to exchange with a partner. *Answers to each clue are provided in parentheses for your easy reference.

1. King Manuel I of Portugal chose me to find a route around Africa to India. *I sailed in 1497 with four ships and 170 men. *(Vasco da Gama)*

2. On April 12, 1961, I became the first person to travel in space. *The *Vostok* 1 travelled at the rate of 8 km per second. *(Yuri Gagarin)*

3. As a Christian missionary, I was sent to Cape Town in South Africa. *I was the first European to see Victoria Falls. *(David Livingstone)*

4. As a 15 year old, I accompanied my father and uncle to China. *I was made a representative of the Kubla Khan's court for 17 years. *(Marco Polo)*

5. In 1325, I set out on a pilgrimage to Mecca. *My caravan used camels for transportation. *(Ibn Battuta)*

6. My father was Eric the Red of Greenland. *After sailing southwest I found Labrador and Vinland. *(Leif Ericsson)*

7. I was the Spanish conquistador who defeated the Aztecs. *Our troops' horses and cannons terrified the Aztecs. *(Hernando Cortes)*

8. I planned 14 expeditions in 12 years, yet I never sailed on any of them. *My men sailed on caravels. *(Prince Henry of Portugal)*

9. As Commander of the *Endeavour*, I took measures to improve the health of my sailors. *My first mission was to Tahiti. *(James Cook)*

10. Inspired by the novel *Robinson Crusoe*, I was the first Frenchman to reach Timbuktu and return. *I stayed in Africa three years to learn Arabic. *(Rene' Caillie')*

11. My real name was John Rowlands. *I was assigned by my newspaper to search Africa to find David Livingstone. *(H.M.Stanley)*

12. After quarreling with the kind of Portugal, I sailed for Spain. *Only the ship, *Vittoria*, reached Spain after circumnavigating the globe. *(Ferdinand Magellan)*

It's All in the Name

Reinforce vocabulary from *The Usborne Book of Explorers* with this lesson. Prepare for this activity by copying the Vocabulary Words on one section on the chalkboard and the Answer Box in another section. Draw a box or circle around each group of words. (If the equipment is available, make a transparency of this page for the overhead projector.) Call on a student to choose a Vocabulary word and draw a line from it to the correct match in the Answer Box. Continue until all words have been matched.

Vocabulary Words

Huitzilpochtli	Silk Road	gauchos
outback	"the smoke that thunders"	"fool's gold"
monsoon	sagas	nomads
bathysphere	dhow	Huns
llanos	Skraelings	"Cabo Tormentoso"
lunks	scurvy	"Green Sea of Darkness"
caravel	Conquistador	kayaks
pampas	*Sputnik 1*	knorr

Answer Box

Portuguese ship	Cape of Storm
Argentinean cowboys	spherical diving machine
Victoria Falls	wandering people
seasonal winds	type of ship used in Africa
Aztec sun god	the first satellite launched into space
Viking ship used for trading expeditions	Norwegian name for Native Americans
disease caused by lack of Vitamin C	fierce tribesman from central Asia
trade route between China and the West	an area at the Equator thought to be dangerous
interior region of Australia	Spanish for conqueror
iron pyrite	tales of Viking exploits
dry, dusty plains	one-man canoes
15th century Chinese ships	plains of Argentina

42

Exploration Word Bank

Some more strategies for expanding and developing vocabulary are presented on this page. A sample vocabulary list is provided but you may want to add other words to it.

Huitzilpochtli	llanos	saffron
Silk Road	Skraelings	Inuits
gauchos	pilgrimage	naturalist
junks	expedition	astronomer
scurvy	missionary	biologist
Buddha	dynasty	linguist
monsoon	caravel	geologist
sagas	Conquistadors	evolution
nomads	kayaks	straits
bathysphere	pampas	chronicles
dhow	imperial	aqualung
Huns	knorr	satellite

Activities

* *Flash Cards.* Cut rectangular pieces of construction paper. Write each vocabulary word on a separate piece and its corresponding definition on the opposite side. Pairs of students can use the cards to quiz one another on definitions or spellings.

* *Display.* Write each vocabulary word on a separate index card. Display the cards on the chalk tray. After a few days, remove one word. Ask students which one is missing. Have them identify and define the missing word.

* *Alphabetize.* Use the index cards from the activity above. With clothespins attach the index cards to a length of yarn suspended from the ceiling. Student pairs or individuals can take turns alphabetizing the list from top to bottom.

* *Crossword Puzzles.* Pair or group the students and supply them with graph paper. Direct them to make a crossword puzzle using at least 16 of the vocabulary words. After checking them, make copies of these student-generated puzzles and use as worksheets.

* *Critical Thinking.* Categorize the words. Give each group of students a copy of the vocabulary words. Tell them to group the words together in categories. For example, dhow, caravel, junks, and knorr are all sailing vessels. Give a prize to the group which can find the most categories for the words.

* *Grammar.* Display the vocabulary list or have students make a copy of the words. Have them identify all the nouns. Direct them to write the plural form of all singular nouns. Identify and list all proper nouns, abstract nouns, or concrete nouns, etc.

Compare and Contrast

Compare and contrast the explorers, Richard Burton and John Speke, who together searched for the source of the Nile River. Although they had traveled together before they were an unusual pair. Read the descriptions below and write them in the proper section of the chart

* suffered from malaria

* at ease among the Arabs

* spoke 29 languages

* a quiet, careful planner

* knew little Arabic

* died in a shooting accident

* led a second expedition to Lake Victoria

* appointed by the Royal Geographic Society of London

* took most of the credit for finding the Nile's source

* his legs became paralyzed

* named his discovery Lake Victoria

* went deaf and blind

* ruthless and determined

* had written numerous books

* appointed leader of the expedition

B U R T O N	
B O T H	
S P E K E	

Impact

The first meetings between the Europeans and the natives of the "new world" resulted in change that profoundly affected both peoples. Some changes benefited the Europeans, but many changes had a negative impact on the Native Americans. Find out more about these changes by reading the paragraph below. Unscramble the groups of letters to make words that will complete the sentence. If you need help, use the Word Bank at the bottom of the page.

Some Europeans became *(eltwayh)*_____ from all the gold,

silver, and furs that they obtained from the *(aivtNe)*._____ Americans.

The European diet changed as new foods such as corn, *(ocaoc)* _____,

and *(mosetato)* _____ were introduced.

The Native Americans, however, did not fare as well. Contagious *(seidases)* _____

were passed on to them by the explorers. *(plamSlxo)* _____ killed

close to *(enysvet - vfie)* _____ percent of the Native Americans who

once inhabited both North and South *(rAicmea)* _____. Many

others died when they were forced to *(bolar)* _____in mines and on farms.

Their lives were changed forever as they acquired European *(solot)*, _____

weapons, and cooking *(slenutis)* _____; began to breed horses,

cows, and *(heicksuc)* _____; and grew wheat and rice.

WORD BANK

diseases	Smallpox	utensils	tomatoes
tools	chickens	wealthy	America
Native	labor	cocoa	seventy-five

Cause and Effect

This exercise is designed to help students analyze why things happen. Also, it is a visual representation of the connections between an event or situation and the reasons for its occurrence. As you study about the explorers, you will find many examples which can be examined by the students. Model the technique with the class before assigning small groups to work independently.

Sample Diagram

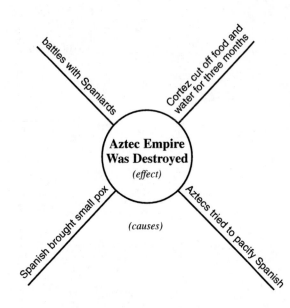

Procedure:

- Draw a simple shape (dome, circle, oval, etc.) on the chalkboard or overhead projector.

- Write an effect inside the shape.

- Brainstorm possible contributing causes with the students.

- Record appropriate responses on the lines (add as many lines as needed).

- Repeat the process using a different effect until students can comfortably work independently on the project. Some sample topics and their causes can be found below.

Sample Topics

- Spices Changed the Quality of Life

    [food could be preserved; improved the flavor of foods; hid the taste and smell of tainted meat]

- The Explorations Changed the World

    [there were new places to settle; natives could be converted to Christianity; new routes were found to remote places; exotic goods could finally be obtained; changed ideas about the size of the world]

- Exploration Flourished

    [advances in technology allowed for more exact sailing; desire for spices, silks, and riches from other countries; wish to spread Christianity; explorers wanted fame, honor, and wealth]

- Columbus' Childhood Encouraged Him to Become an Explorer

    [his weaver father sailed to distant cities; Columbus learned as much as he could on these voyages; Columbus questioned others' knowledge about the sea and the world; worked as a paid seaman; lived on the Mediterranean]

- Vasco Nuñez de Balboa Became an Explorer

    [escaped to South America to hide from his debts; heard about the immensely rich Incas; thought he'd be safe if he did something important]

Three of a Kind

On the chalkboard or overhead projector, copy the list of Categories from the box below. (Omit this step if your students are up for a real challenge). Introduce students to the task by asking them what the following three names have in common—Lenin Peak, Mt. Everest, and Annapurna. Establish that they are the names of mountains. Specifically, they are three of the highest mountains in the world.

Read aloud each Word Group below the Categories Box. Have the students identify the category. (For your easy reference answers are provided in parentheses.)

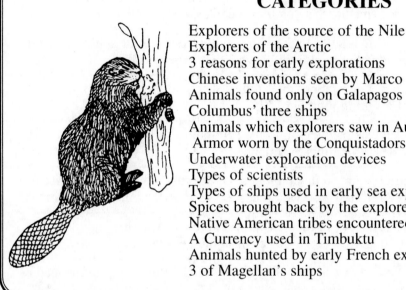

CATEGORIES

Explorers of the source of the Nile
Explorers of the Arctic
3 reasons for early explorations
Chinese inventions seen by Marco Polo
Animals found only on Galapagos
Columbus' three ships
Animals which explorers saw in Australia
Armor worn by the Conquistadors
Underwater exploration devices
Types of scientists
Types of ships used in early sea explorations
Spices brought back by the explorers
Native American tribes encountered by Lewis and Clark
A Currency used in Timbuktu
Animals hunted by early French explorers
3 of Magellan's ships

WORD GROUPS

1. Marine iguana, giant tortoise, Galapagos finch (animals found only on Galapagos)
2. saffron, ginger, cinnamon (spices brought back by the explorers)
3. Mandan, Clatsop, Missouri (Native American tribes encountered by Lewis and Clark)
4. naturalist, biologist, geologist (types of scientists)
5. *Vittoria, Trinidad, San Antonio* (3 of Magellan's ships)
6. Robert Peary, Fridtjof Nanse, Roald Amundsen (explorers of the Arctic)
7. aqualung, FNRS3, bathysphere (underwater exploration devices)
8. cowrie shells, iron chain, copper ingot (currency used in Timbuktu)
9. *Niña, Santa María, Pinta* (Columbus' three ships)
10. Richard Burton, James Grant, John Speke (explorers of the source of the Nile)
11. paper money, gunpowder, stamp for printing (Chinese inventions seen by Marco Polo)
12. chain mail, bronze helmet, battle axe (armor worn by the Conquistadors)
13. otter, beaver, marten (animals hunted by early French explorers)
14. dhow, caravel, knorr (types of ships used in early sea explorations)
15. trade, treasures, religion (3 reasons for early explorations)
16. rainbow lorikeet, goanna, wallaby (animals explorers saw in Australia)

Creative Writing Topics

Here are some suggested ways for using the creative writing topics below.

1. Write one topic per day on the chalkboard; have students write for a specified amount of time.

2. Present students with three or four topics from which to choose.

3. Provide students with a copy of all the topics for homework; determine a due date for each one.

4. Cut apart the rectangles, place into a bag, and have students draw one.

---

* In Columbus' day people thought there were monsters, giants, and mermaids in the ocean. Draw a picture and write a paragraph about a sea creature that you think people then might have imagined.

---

* You are a fifteenth century explorer. Write a letter to the King and Queen of your country; outline your reasons for wanting to explore unknown regions. Tell what you expect to find.

---

* When Columbus was in Iceland he heard tales about the Vikings who had voyaged into the western seas. Write your own tale of a Viking journey.

---

* The thick seaweed of the Sargasso Sea was frightening to the sailors in Columbus' fleet. Pretend you are a sailor. Write a letter home describing this experience.

---

* When the *Santa María* hit a reef and was wrecked, Columbus had to leave 43 men behind because there was no room on the other ships. Tell how you would choose 43 men if you were Columbus.

---

* Spanish conquistadors believed that they were entitled to the resources of America regardless of who lived there. Write a paragraph telling why you agree or disagree with this philosophy.

---

* You are an astronaut. Explain how the early explorers of Christopher Columbus' era influenced your decision to become an astronaut.

---

* The year is 1498 and you are the first female explorer. Write a story about your all-female crew and their important discovery.

---

* Tell what would be more exciting to you: to be an explorer in the late fifteenth to early sixteenth century or to be an astronaut on a mission to the moon. Explain the reasons for your choice.

---

* Compare the dangers faced by early explorers and those faced by current space explorers. Which would you rather have to deal with and why?

---

* You are the gromet on the late night shift. Half way through you fall asleep. When you awaken you see that the sand has stopped flowing. The captain walks in. Finish this scene.

---

* What if Columbus and Leonardo da Vinci had met? Write a conversation they might have had. (Think about some things they might have had in common.)

---

* Pretend you are Magellan. Instead of sailing around the world, your voyage takes you to the future (1990's). How would you and your crew react to all the new technology? Write a story.

---

* What one modern technological advance in navigation would the explorers of the late 1400's to late 1500's find the most beneficial? Which advance would surprise them the most?

---

* Write a story telling about a voyage that Cortes and Pizarro might have planned together. Do you think they would have gotten along well or would there have been arguments?

---

* Choose any two explorers. Compare their characteristics and personality traits. Which traits most helped them complete their journeys?

A Math Lab

For a change of pace conduct a math lab. Cut apart the task cards below and place one at each table or group of desks. Divide the students into small groups and have them number a sheet of paper from 1 to 12. Assign each group a specific table at which to begin and establish the pattern of movement. Direct the students to solve the problem at their table. At a given signal have the students move to the next table and solve the new problem. Continue in this manner until all problems have been solved. Review the solutions and answers together. **Note:** You may have students work independently, if you prefer.

1. Ibn Battuta's travels through Africa, the Middle East, and the Far East covered 75,000 miles. How many yards is that?	7. On one of his journeys Hsuan-tsang was accompanied by a huge elephant that ate 40 bundles of hay each day. At that rate how many bundles of hay did the elephant eat in one month (based on 30 days)?
2. Mungo Park's journey began with 30 soldiers and ten other Europeans. By the time they had reached the Niger, 29 had died of disease and exhaustion. How many were still living?	8. In 1497 Vasco de Gama sailed with four ships and 170 men. If the man were equally divided among the ships how many would be on each ship? How many would be left over?
3. Columbus thought the Indies were 3,500 miles to the west but they were actually 16,000 miles. What is the difference between Columbus' estimate and the actual distance?	9. Lewis and Clark's journey took them over a distance of 12,000 km during two and a half years. How many miles did they travel, on average, each year?
4. H.M. Stanley returned to Africa in 1874. At the end of the expedition 114 of the original 356 members remained. How many had died or deserted?	10. In the 18th century an average of 60 out of 100 sailors died on long voyages. Write this as a fraction. Reduce it to its lowest terms. Write it as a percentage.
5. When David Livingstone died his faithful companions embalmed his body and carried it to Zanzibar. This 8-month journey was 1609 km. On the average, how many km did they travel each day?	11. On April 12, 1961, Yuri Gagarin became the first person to travel in space. His spacecraft's speed during the 108-minute trip was 5 meters per second. How many miles did he travel altogether?
6. Chang Ch'ien set out in 138 B.C. to make an alliance with the Yeuchi. He was gone 12 years. What year was it when he returned?	12. Jacques Piccard, seven-mile descent to the ocean floor took five hours. At that rate how long would it take to descend 28 miles.

Voyage Math

Solve each problem below. Then write the answer in the blank to learn some intriguing facts about the early explorers and their voyages.

1. 25 x 140 Columbus thought the distance between Spain and the Indies was only _____ miles.	7. 434 ÷ 7 Hernán Cortés died at the age of _____.
2. 224 ÷ 16 da Gama led _____ warships to battle the Arab fleet.	8. 102 ÷ 6 Marco Polo and his family stayed in China for _____ years.
3. 50 x 5 Magellan led a fleet of _____ men through the Strait of Magellan.	9. 270 ÷ 3 Pizarro received more than _____ million dollars in gold and silver from the Incas.
4. 152 ÷ 4 It took Magellan _____ days to pass through the strait.	10. 144 ÷ 12 The *Santa María* was only _____ feet wide.
5. 5 x 83 Cortes and his _____ soldiers and horsemen amazed the Tlascalans.	11. 25 x 10 Only 18 of the _____ men survived Magellan's voyage around the world.
6. 520 ÷ 13 Columbus was _____ years old when he began his first voyage in 1492.	12. 5 x 16 The *Santa María* was 70 or _____ feet long.

Explorers' Riches

The explorers returned from their voyages with many interesting things. Some brought back foods and cloth that the Europeans desired, new foods they'd never seen, exotic animals, and precious metals. To find out the names of some of these products, begin at the arrow and draw a continuous line through the letters in each box to spell a word (see example). Write each product name below the box. Use the Word Bank and number of blank spaces to help you.

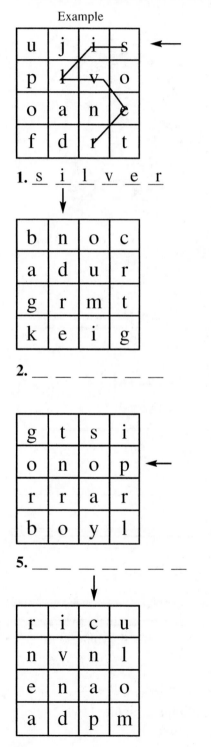

Example

1. s i l v e r

Word Bank

silks	pepper
parrots	sweet potatoes
pineapples	nutmeg
cinnamon	tobacco
maize	

b	n	o	c
a	d	u	r
g	r	m	t
k	e	i	g

2. _ _ _ _ _ _ _

o	c	l	f
t	c	a	i
g	n	r	b
a	g	t	o

3. _ _ _ _ _ _ _ _

s	i	p	p
p	n	a	l
a	e	e	r
r	t	s	o

4. _ _ _ _ _ _ _ _ _ _

g	t	s	i
o	n	o	p
r	r	a	r
b	o	y	l

5. _ _ _ _ _ _ _

s	t	s	o
w	e	p	t
e	t	t	a
r	o	e	s

6. _ _ _ _ _
   _ _ _ _ _ _ _ _

o	p	b	r
p	c	n	e
r	e	p	l
c	a	p	i

7. _ _ _ _ _ _ _

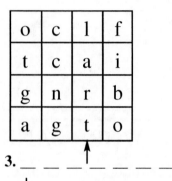

r	i	c	u
n	v	n	l
e	n	a	o
a	d	p	m

8. _ _ _ _ _ _ _ _

f	n	i	s
s	c	l	e
a	k	o	r
t	e	g	f

9. _ _ _ _ _

z	l	m	a
b	a	d	r
i	g	k	f
c	z	e	s

10. _ _ _ _ _ _

Spanish and Aztec Armor

Label the Spanish and the Aztec armor in the chart below with terms from the Word Bank. Then answer the questions that follow.

WORD BANK

cane-shield	chain-mail	bronze helmet	wooden club
breastplate		cotton suit	sword

Answer the questions on the lines provided.

1. Which culture's armor offered the most protection?_____

    Why? _____

2. Why did the Aztec weapons terrify the Spaniards? _____.

    _____

3. What two things did Cortés army have that the Aztecs didn't? (**Hint:** The Aztecs had never seen either one.) _____

4. If you were a Spanish soldier and could have only one piece of the armor pictured, what would you choose and why?_____

    _____

5. If you were an Aztec warrior and could have only one piece of the equipment pictured, what would you choose and why? _____

    _____

Explorer Art

The art projects outlined below can be incorporated into your explorers unit at anytime. They may be completed as individual or group activities.

All That Glitters

Materials: gold and silver glitter; glue bottle with spout; waxed paper; nylon or metallic thread
Directions:

- Place the waxed paper on a flat surface.

- With the glue draw a thick outline of a design onto the waxed paper. Designs should be related to the explorers and natives. Some examples are masks, weapons, and gold pieces.

- Completely cover the outlines with gold or silver glitter.

- After drying thoroughly (at least overnight), carefully peel away the waxed paper.

- Hang the shapes up with nylon or metallic thread.

Golden Collage

Materials: old magazines; glue; scissors; tagboard or poster board
Directions:

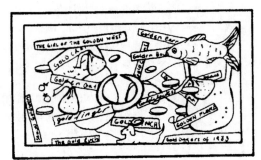

- Look through old magazines for pictures of things that are gold. Also look for words and phrases about gold.

- Cut out the pictures, words, and phrases.

- Arrange the cut-outs on the tagboard until you are pleased with the design.

- Glue the cut-outs to the tagboard.

- As an alternative, make a silver collage.

Golden Etching

Materials: gold wax crayons; black poster paint; paintbrush; nail file or paper clip, straightened; small pieces of white construction paper or poster board

Directions:
- With the wax crayon completely cover the paper.

- With the black poster paint cover the crayoned paper. (You may need to use more than one coat of poster paint.)

- Allow the paint to dry. With a nail file or paper clip (or other sharp-edged object) scratch off a shape or design.

Note: For a silver etching, color the paper with a silver wax crayon.

Alternate technique: Cover the paper with a thick coating of white candle wax by rubbing the candle across the page. Paint the page with gold or silver poster paint. After drying, scratch off a shape or design.

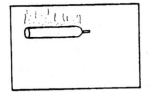

Coat of Arms Big Book

Have the students write stories or reports on a coat of arms cut-out. How-to's follow. Choose the method that is best-suited to your class needs.

Copier Method

- Block this text with paper cut to fit inside this coat of arms pattern.

- Attach the paper cut-out to the pattern with a dab of glue in the center of the pattern.

- Copy on the copy machine making as many as will be needed.

Template

- Make a template. Cut out this pattern and glue to tagboard or poster board. Cut out the tagboard or poster board.

- Direct the students to place the template on their paper, trace around the shape, and cut it out.

- Have them make as many shape pages as they will need.

Tracing

- Place a sheet of thin, white paper over this page.
- With a pencil, trace the bold outline.
- Cut out, and use the cut-out as a guide for making more pages.

Suggested Uses

Group students to work on any of the following projects:
- Write a book titled My Life as an Explorer.
- Write an in-depth report focusing on one explorer.
- Write a report about the parallels between exploration in the 1400-1500's and current space exploration.
- Write a book about all the instruments that Columbus used to navigate.
- Write an explorer's alphabet, e.g. A is for Arawak, B is for Balboa.
- Make original coats of arms for their family names.

A Spicy Affair

As a culminating activity, host a spice fair in which students learn about spices as they participate in various projects. Small groups or pairs may work together on some projects, but individuals may want their own spice necklace or picture. Activities may be worked on throughout the week, and on the designated day all projects should be displayed. Invite another class or the principal to come and enjoy a spice-filled event. Directions for each activity are outlined below. Pick and choose those that are most appropriate for your class.

Glue and Spice Pictures

Materials: white glue; selection of spices such as paprika, pepper, cinnamon, nutmeg, and powdered mustard; drawing paper; pencil

Directions:
- With pencil draw a simple picture on the paper. (Inca and Aztec designs would be very appropriate.)
- Spread glue on the picture one area at a time.
- Cover the glue with a spice; gently shake off excess.
- Repeat both former steps until the entire surface is covered.

Spice Jewelry

Materials: whole spices such as cloves and allspice; bowl of water; needle; nylon thread or dental floss

Directions:

- Soak the spices in water overnight, or until they are soft.
- Thread the needle with nylon or dental floss.
- Pierce the spices onto the thread in any pattern desired. (Depending on the length of the chain a necklace, bracelet, or anklet can be made.)
- Tie the ends together securely in a knot.

Spiced Dough

Materials: flour; salt; water; measuring cups; bowl; variety of spices; cookie sheet; oven

Directions:
- In a bowl, mix 2 cups of flour, $\frac{1}{2}$ cup of salt, $\frac{3}{4}$ cup of water, and any amount of spices by hand.
- Knead for a few minutes until the dough is firm.
- Form dough artifacts, jewelry, or ornaments.
- Place on the cookie sheet and bake at 350° F for 12 minutes or until hard.

Research Boards

Materials: poster board; self-sealing plastic bags; spices; stapler

Directions:
- Assign each pair of students a different spice.
- Have them research the plant from which it originates, its history, country of origin, and common use.
- Tell them to fill a plastic bag about $\frac{1}{4}$ full of their assigned spice.
- Attach the bag to the poster board with staples.
- Direct the students to draw a picture of the plant and write their research data in a format similar to the illustration above.
- Display all the research boards on the chalk tray or a special bulletin board.

A Spicy Affair *(cont.)*

Sniff Test

Materials: empty margarine cups; cotton balls; spices; knife or ice pick; markers; tagboard strips

Directions:

- For each margarine cup you will need three or four cotton balls.
- Sprinkle a group of cotton balls liberally with one spice (for example, vanilla).
- Put the cotton into a cup and cover with a plastic lid that has four or five air holes (made by poking a knife or ice pick through the lid).
- Repeat the two former steps until all the margarine cups have been filled.
- With the marker write a different spice name on each tagboard strip.
- Place the cups in a row on a table.
- Mix up the tagboard strips and place in a pile next to the cups.
- Direct the students to sniff the contents of each cup and place the correct label in front of the appropriate cup.
- When one students is finished testing, mix up the cards and the order of the cups.

Spiced Cookies

Ingredients:

1 egg	1¾ c. (400 mL) all-purpose flour
⅓ c. (75 mL) shortening	1 teaspoon (5 mL) baking powder
⅓ c. (75 mL) margarine	½ teaspoon (2 mL) salt
¾ c. (150 mL) sugar	1 teaspoon (5 mL) vanilla

Directions:

- Slightly beat the egg in a mixing bowl.
- Add the remaining ingredients and blend with a spoon.
- With your hands form the dough into a ball. (Add 1 or 2 tablespoons of milk if the dough doesn't stick together.)
- Mold the dough into shapes (serpent, sun, etc.).
- Coat one side of each cookie with the nut/spice mixture.
- Place cookies on ungreased cookie sheet.
- Bake at 375°F (190°C) for about ten minutes. Yield: 2 dozen cookies.

> **Nut/Spice Coating**
> Mix 1/3 c. (75 mL) finely chopped pecans, 2 tablespoons (30 mL) sugar and 2 tablespoons (30 mL) cinnamon.

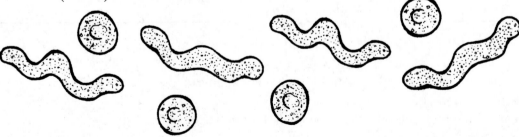

A Challenging Crossword

This challenging crossword puzzle will be easy for those who have researched Columbus and other early explorers. Some clues have been provided to help you.

Across

3. This Portuguese naval officer was the first to sail completely around the world.

5. America was named after this astronomer.

8. An obedient servant of the King; he had Columbus put in chains.

9. Lateen sails were triangular; these sails were square.

12. The Native Americans surprised Columbus by smoking this.

14. A disease caused by lack of vitamin C; many sailors suffered from this.

15. The sailors sang this hymn of prayer every evening.

16. He was the ruler of China during the thirteenth century.

17. This explorer traveled to China 2 centuries before Columbus' voyage.

Down

1. The explorer who was first to circumnavigate Africa to reach India.

2. These two brothers commanded the *Niña* and the *Pinta*.

4. Imaginary east-west parallel lines around the globe.

6. The compass needle always points north to the Polaris Star.

7. In 1513 this Spanish explorer found the Pacific Ocean.

8. The islands on which Columbus actually landed in 1492.

10. Columbus promised a silken jacket to the first one who saw land. Another name for this silken jacket.

11. This was the occupation of Columbus' family.

13. This prince, nicknamed the Navigator, established a school for Mariners.

Explorers Word Banks

This resource page is a handy reference for various writing activities such as reports, creative writing, rhymes and poems, social studies lessons, and science experiments. In addition, these words can be used as spelling word lists and can serve as a springboard for brainstorming.

Bodies of Water

Mediterranean Sea

Strait of Magellan

Atlantic Ocean

Indian Ocean

Pacific Ocean

South Sea

Caribbean Sea

Ships

Niña

Pinta

Santa María

Victoria

Trinidad

Sea Terms

journal	caravel
log books	astrolabe
prime meridian	equator
sea monsters	knots
compass	leagues
latitude	North Star
longitude	cross-staff
International Date Line	lateen
dead reckoning	carracks

Explorers

Vasco Núñez de Balboa	Francisco Pizarro	Henry Hudson
Christopher Columbus	Hernán Cortés	Francis Drake
Marco Polo	Vasco da Gama	Bartholomeu Dias
Giovanni daVerrazano	Amerigo Vespucci	Samuel de Champlain
Ferdinand Magellan	Vikings	

Countries and Cultures

Peru

Incas

Mexico

Aztecs

South America

Spain

Portugal

Italy

Hispaniola

Native American

Cuba

Cipangu

Arawaks

Bahamas

Africa

Important People

Queen Isabella	Prince Henry the Navigator
King Ferdinand	Rustichello
Kubla Khan	King John II
Lady Marina	Pedranas
Almagro	Diego Columbus
Montezuma	Luis de Santangel
Martin Alonzo	Bartholomew Las Casas
Atahualpo	Ptolemy

Terms

"horse-men"	contagious	conquistador
smallpox	"New World"	scurvy
expansion	technology	expedition
Christianity	Polaris	doublet

Stores on Board

When Columbus set sail for the Indies, he made sure there were enough stores on board to last a year. Vessels carried **wine, water, sardines, anchovies, cheese, chick peas, lentils, beans, rice, honey, almonds, raisins, biscuits, garlic, oil, and vinegar.**

Fill in the puzzle spaces below with the names of the 16 foods stored on board. Some clues have been given to help you.

Answer the questions on the lines provided.

1. Of the foods named in the puzzle, write the ones you have tasted.

_____

_____

_____

2. Of the foods named in the puzzle, write the ones you have not tasted.

_____

_____

_____

3. Of the foods named in the puzzle, write the ones you like best.

_____

_____

_____

Ordeal on the High Seas

When Magellan's surviving crew returned to Spain from their voyage around the world, they spoke of nightmarish conditions including spoiled food, scurvy, and lack of fresh foods. Of the five ships and 250 men who began the journey, only one ship, the *Victoria*, with 18 men returned to Seville. Magellan had been well-prepared for the voyage (see the chart below, left), but many unexpected factors contributed to the high death rate. The fresh oranges and lemons were eaten within the first few weeks. Then the wine soured and turned into vinegar (which the men drank anyway). Rats, worms, lice, and weevils infested and ruined the remaining food. For more than three months the crewman had to endure unsanitary, unsafe, and unfresh foods.

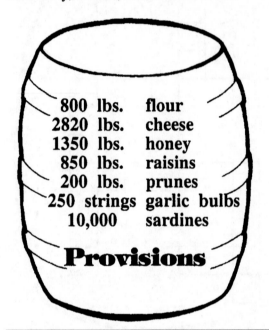

800 lbs.	flour	
2820 lbs.	cheese	
1350 lbs.	honey	
850 lbs.	raisins	
200 lbs.	prunes	
250 strings	garlic bulbs	
10,000	sardines	

Provisions

Take a look at a list of some of the provisions that Magellan brought on board. Then answer the questions below. Workspace has been provided for you to use.

1. How many pounds of flour, cheese, honey, raisins, and prunes were there altogether?

   Total Pounds_____

2. There were 250 crewmen. How many pounds of food each would they be alotted? (Hint: Use the Total Pounds from the previous problem.)

   Pounds Allotted Each _____

3. Ten thousand sardines were provided. If each crewmen ate the same number of sardines, how many did each man eat?

   Sardines for Each Man_____

4. If each string of garlic contained 12 bulbs, how many bulbs were there altogether?

   Garlic Bulbs Altogether _____

Name _____

Volcanic Reactions

A *volcano* is an opening in the earth's crust. *Ashes*, hot gases, *lava* and pieces of *rock* erupt through this opening when underground *magma chambers* become heated. Lava is a *molten*, or liquid, form of rock that flows down the side of a volcano in *fiery* rivers. As it cools the lava hardens into various *formations*. Although many volcanoes are *cone-shaped*, some are *fissures*, or cracks, in the ground. Volcanoes may occur on *continents*, on *islands*, at the bottom of the sea, and even on some *planets* other than earth. These eruptions are often *violent* and result in the loss of many lives and widespread destruction of *property*.

central vent →

Directions: Read the paragraph about volcanoes, left. Then label the diagram using some of the bold words in the paragraph. Finally, find all of the bold words in the word search below. Words may be found across, down, diagonal, or backwards.

Challenge: Find out about some famous volcanoes such as Mt. Vesuvius, Mt. St. Helens, Krakatau, or Mt. Kilauea.

```
Y E N R I Q U V A L A P A M O L T E N C
T D A V A I F O R M A T I O N S A A D O
R A D I C A A L A R A S A D R A C K A N
E A S E A T A C A R E E D A G A P C A E
P A Y A W A S A Z A Q H A N A V A O A S
O F C R A T A N S J A S A M A K A R A H
R A P A E A O O A H A L A J A L A K A A
P A P N A I I A C A E A G A S A S A H P
A W A N A Q F R A M E S E A S E A I A E
H L O C K E S R E B M A H C A M G A M D
P A V I O L E N T Y I S F U N A N D E A
X C I T I N G T H E A D F I S S U R E S
W A A V A L N E G R R E E T Z Y G R A N
T F U H R S T N E N I T N O C W F U H A
```

Voyage to the Moon

Exploration continues today in outer space. But years ago people only dreamed of traveling in space. Supposedly, Alexander the Great used two griffins—fictitious animals that were half lion, half eagle—to power a space craft. In 1768 Italian scientist Bernardo Zamagna invented a balloon-boat that he thought could carry men to the moon. Jules Verne wrote a book about a moon train in 1865. But it wasn't until 1957 that these dreams became realities. That year, on November 3rd, Russia launched the first space traveler, a dog named Laika. Unfortunately, Laika died in space because there was no way to return her to earth. Advances were made and on April 12, 1961, Russian cosmonaut Yuri Gagarin became the first human to travel in outer space. America put astronaut Alan Shepard in space on May 5, 1961. Nine months later John Glenn orbited the earth three times.

Starting in 1965, the U.S. launched its Gemini program. During these 12 flights, astronauts practiced hooking up their spacecraft with others. Space flights were becoming longer, and in 1968 *Apollo 8* orbited the moon ten times. These flights paved the way for the most astounding feat to date: On July 20, 1969, astronauts Neil Armstrong and Edwin Aldrin became the first men to walk on the moon.

Discover Armstrong's historic words as he first stepped onto the moon's surface. Solve the math problems below: Find the answer in the box and write that letter on the blank. One has been done to help you.

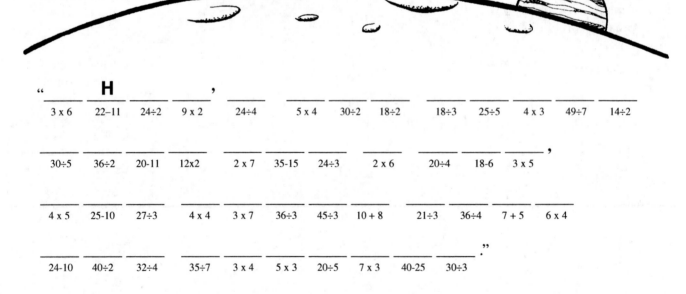

" __ **H** __ __ __ ,
  3 x 6 22–11 24÷2 9 x 2   24÷4   5 x 4   30÷2 18÷2   18÷3   25÷5   4 x 3   49÷7   14÷2

__ __ __ __   __ __ __ __   __ __ __ ,
30÷5 36÷2 20-11 12x2   2 x 7 35-15 24÷3   2 x 6   20÷4 18-6 3 x 5

__ __ __ __ __ __ __   __ __ __ __
4 x 5 25-10 27÷3 4 x 4 3 x 7 36÷3 45÷3 10 + 8   21÷3 36÷4 7 + 5 6 x 4

__ __ __ __ __ __ __ __ __ __ ."
24-10 40÷2 32÷4   35÷7 3 x 4 5 x 3 20÷5 7 x 3 40-25 30÷3

Answer Box

S = 6	F = 14	H = 11	G = 16	R = 8	P = 24
N = 15	T = 18	O = 20	A = 12	M = 5	K = 4
	E = 9	L = 7	D = 10	I = 21	

Meteor and Comet Venn Diagram

Complete the comet and meteor Venn diagram by writing each statement below in the correct section of the intersecting circles.

- are members of the solar system
- tails are millions of miles long
- appear in the night sky for many days
- are made of iron and stone
- have a tail

- fall quickly to earth
- are called "shooting stars"
- orbit around the sun
- hardly made of anything
- some are visible without telescopes

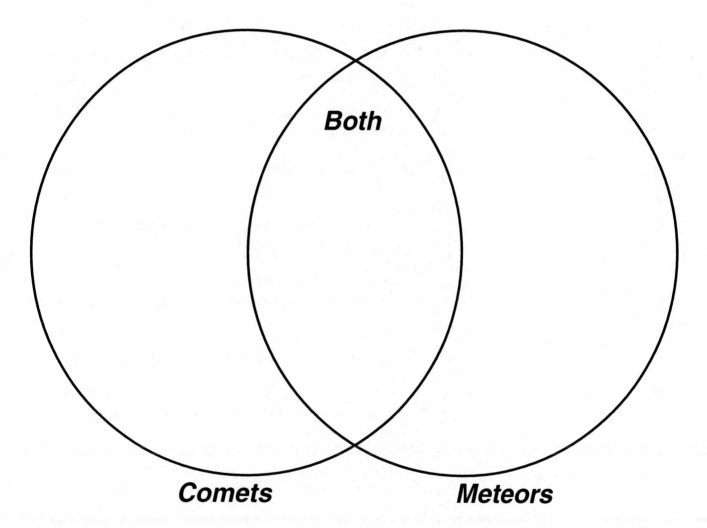

Both

Comets   **Meteors**

Challenge: Meteor showers are caused when broken meteors fly by the Earth. They can best be seen after midnight on a moonless night away from city lights and obstructions. Plan to watch for meteors with a friend. Lie down head to head so that each one of you can observe half of the sky. Best dates for viewing meteor showers and their length of visibility are: May 5 (18 days); October 21 (8 days); November 16 (4 days); December 13 (6 days).

Who's Who

Many famous people besides Columbus were alive sometime during the late 1400's and mid 1500's. Each made a memorable contribution to history and their stories are still told today. See how many of the historical figures and events you can put together. Names can be found in the Name Bank at the bottom of the page. Use reference materials to help you.

1._____ This Renaissance painter is famous for his *Mona Lisa*. In addition, he was an architect, engineer, and inventor.

2._____ When the Pope refused his request for a divorce from his wife, Catherine, this English king formed his own church.

3 _____ Thanks to his invention of movable type, different books can be printed with the same press.

4._____ His theory that the earth and other planets orbit around the sun revolutionized the science of astronomy.

5._____ An italian statesman, he wrote *The Prince*, a famous guide to using political power.

6._____ A sculptor, painter, and architect, he is famous for his painting in the Sistine Chapel.

7._____ Known as the "Queen of Scots," she persecuted Protestants in order to make England Catholic again.

8._____ Notoriously cruel, this man was the first tsar of Russia. He conquered Siberia and established trading with Europe.

9._____ This former priest disagreed with many things the Catholic Church was doing. His theories and teachings led to the formation of a new church.

10._____ From 1516-1556 he was king of Spain and Holy Roman Emperor. He encourage exploration in the Americas.

Name Bank

Martin Luther	Mary Stuart	Copernicus	Michelangelo	Machiavelli
Johann Gütenberg	Charles V	Henry VIII	Leonardo da Vinci	Ivan the Terrible

The *Santa María*

Label the flagship with the following: crow's nest, Captain's cabin, the hold, deck, lateen sail, redonda sail. Draw supplies in the hold, a boy in the lookout, three men on deck, and a cross on the main sail.

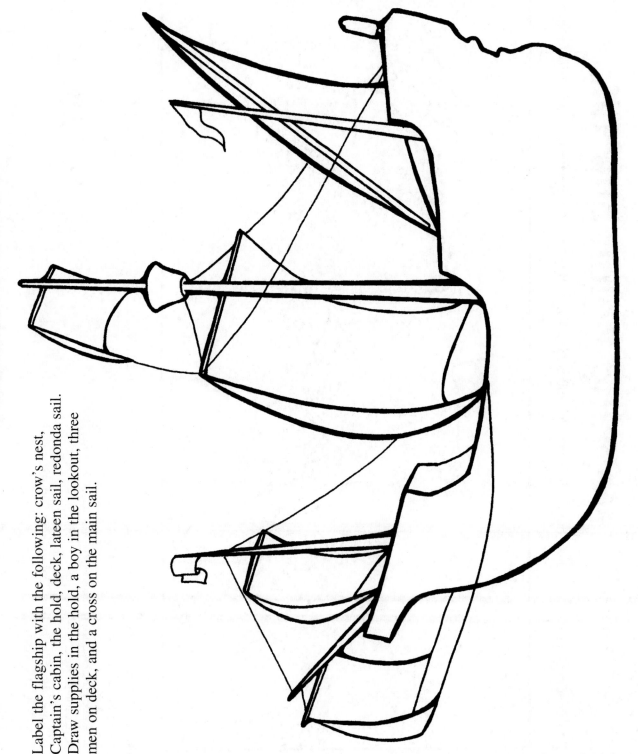

Mapping Columbus' Life

Follow the directions below to map out Christopher Columbus' life. You will need a pencil and colored pencils for this activity.

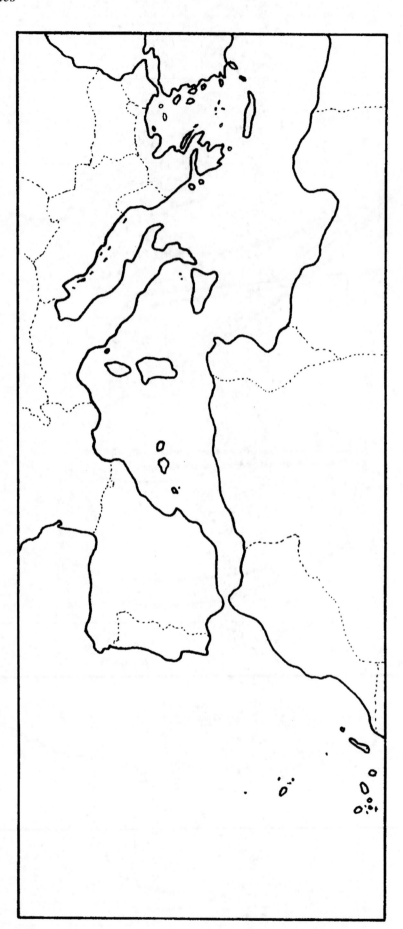

1. Label Italy, the country where Columbus was born in 1451. Make a red X on Genoa, his birthplace.

2. Label the Mediterranean Sea where Columbus learned to sail. Color it blue.

3. Label Portugal where Columbus lived from 1476–1485. Make a purple dot to show Lisbon.

4. Label Spain. Draw a yellow star to indicate Palos from which he sailed west to the Indies.

5. Label Africa. Color it green.

6. Label the Canary Islands off the coast of Africa. Color Teneriffe, where he saw a volcano, brown.

7. Columbus died in 1506 in Spain. Color Spain purple.

8. Draw a compass rose to show north, south, east, and west.

New Explorers

Although the last lands on earth were discovered in 1948, there are still many areas open for exploration. Mountains, seas, the North and South Poles, and the jungles all contain wonders that are just waiting to be explored. Due to advanced technology, specialized tools enable adventurers to carry out their quests more efficiently and scientifically. Dangers still abound, however, adding to the challenge of each journey. Read about some modern explorations below. Research the answers to the questions to learn even more about each one.

Exploring the Oceans

Before the twentieth century, underwater exploration was limited to diving for pearls and natural sponges. It wasn't until breathing apparatus was invented that the ocean was able to be observed. Bathyspheres and bathyscapes allowed people to travel in deep waters. With the invention of the aqua lung, a new era of underwater exploration was begun. Divers were free to swim around, photograph marine life, and collect ocean artifacts.

* What is a bathysphere? a bathyscape?

* What contributions has Jacques Cousteau made to underwater exploration?

Climbing Mountains

Years ago, people feared mountains. Some even worshipped them. However, not until the last 200 years did people begin climbing them. Because proper equipment did not exist, mountain climbing was a very dangerous business. Early climbers simply wore warmer versions of their everyday clothing. These climbers were also limited in the height they could climb, since oxygen in tanks was not available yet. To date, the highest mountain in the world was conquered on May 29, 1953.

* Where is Mt. Everest? How tall is it?

* What contributions has Horace de Saussure make to modern mountaineering?

Racing for the Poles

Both the North and the South Pole are extremely hostile environments, but that did not deter men from trying to be first to reach either pole. Norway's Fridtjof Nansen failed in his voyage, but in 1909 Robert Peary claimed to have reached the North Pole. In 1911 Roald Admundsen competed with Robert Scott's team to reach the South Pole. Admunsen's team was more efficient with its husky dogs and reached the South Pole on December 14, 1911. Tragically the Scott team died of frostbite after reaching the pole in January 1912.

* Explain how Scott's choice of equipment led to his team's death.

* Name some animals found at each pole.

Mapping the Interior

Little was known about the interior of Australia until there was a political push to install telegraph lines across the continent. A government prize offer for the first to travel south to north encouraged a lavish expedition led by Robert Burke and William Wills. Their lack of experience and knowledge of the outback led to their deaths. In 1862 John McDouall and party successfully returned from their journey across the mostly desert area.

* What were some of the hardships endured by the Burke-Wills party?

* Make a list of some of the plant and animal life of the outback.

Critical Thinking Skills

Develop critical thinking skills with this activity. Divide the students into small groups. Supply each group with at least one copy of the story and questions below. Direct the students to read Marco Polo's story. On another sheet of paper have them write answers to the questions. When all the groups have completed the assignment, review the answers in whole group.

Marco Polo's Story

Marco Polo's adventure began some two hundred years before Christopher Columbus voyaged to the New World. Marco was only 12 when he set out with his father and his uncle to visit China. It was a three-year journey filled with wondrous sights, including geysers that pumped out hot oil, and sheep with four-foot curled horns. Young Marco carefully observed the different people they encountered and their religions, customs, and methods of farming. When the Polos reached Kubla Khan's court, they were warmly welcomed, but Khan was especially impressed with Marco. The Khan employed Marco as a representative of the royal court and sent him on many diplomatic missions. For 17 years the Polos stayed in China, but when they wanted to leave the Khan was reluctant to give up his faithful servants. Fortunately, a diplomatic mission supplied them with a way out. After escorting a Mongol princess to her husband-to-be, they escaped. Three years later they arrived in Venice. All in all they had been gone 24 years. Marco Polo's adventures were later recorded in a book titled *The Travels of Marco Polo*. Some people thought Marco had made up his stories because they seemed too farfetched. Others, including Christopher Columbus, were inspired by these tales of another world.

Knowledge: What sights did Marco see during his journey to China? Which Polo did the Khan favor? What did Marco do in China? How long did the Polos stay in China?

Comprehension: Explain how the Polos escaped China after living there so long. Construct a pictorial time line that summarizes events in their story.

Application: Write about what Marco Polo would observe and record if instead of reaching China he'd reached your home. What special experiences or adventures have you had that you could describe for others.

Analysis: Make a list of words or phrases that would describe Marco Polo. Explain why you think the Polos were brave.

Synthesis: Pretend you are Marco Polo; write a letter home describing one day's adventures. Tell what you would have done if the plan to accompany the princess and then escape had failed.

Evaluation: Would Marco's story inspire you to travel to unknown lands? Why or why not? Do you think Marco Polo actually experienced these adventures? Why or why not?

16th Century Art

While Columbus and other explorers were finding new lands and sea routes, artists of the Renaissance were flourishing throughout Europe. Two men were particularly gifted and creative and both were from Italy: Leonardo da Vinci and Michelangelo Buonarroti. Their impact and influence can still be felt in our art, architecture, and thinking today. Introduce students to these very talented men through any of the following projects.

Leonardo da Vinci

- This artist, architect, engineer, and inventor lived from 1452 to 1519. His diverse interests also included time to study music and science. Have the students read a biography about da Vinci and make a list of all his accomplishments.

- Study da Vinci's *Mona Lisa.* Observe how it is organized in a pyramid design. Note the dramatic contrasts of dark and light. Look at some of his other works; find the pyramid and contrasts in them.

- Have the students draw a portrait. Invite a guest to pose for the class or let the students find pictures in books or magazines to copy. For a step-by-step description of the process, see Teacher Created Materials #018 *Masterpiece of the Month.* Another fine resource is *Leonardo Da Vinci's Advice to Artists* edited by Emery Kellen (Thomas Nelson, Inc., 1974).

- Many of Leonardo's ideas were far ahead of their time. He drew plans for a flying machine and a parachute. Also, he believed that the sun did not move. Scientists then believed that the sun revolved around the earth. Have the students research what we now know about the movement of the sun and the planets.

- da Vinci did not use the fresco technique to paint the wall with *The Last Supper.* Direct the students to find out what fresco painting is and why Leonardo rejected its use.

Michelangelo Buonarotti

- Michelangelo was an artist, sculptor, architect, and poet. Mostly he was interested in creating large marble statues. Michelangelo lived from 1475-1564. If possible, show the film *The Agony and the Ecstasy* or read sections from the book of the same title to learn about him.

- Take a field trip to a museum, park, or any other area that has his statues. Note the details and the materials used to make the structures. Find out what material Michelangelo used.

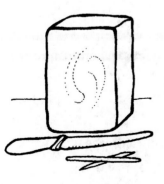

- Give students a carving experience. Each should have a bar of soap and some carving tools such as toothpicks, small kitchen knife, nail file, or wood craft sticks that have been sharpened to a point. Direct the students to create a three-dimensional figure.

- Michelangelo built scaffolding so that he could reach and paint the ceiling of the Sistine Chapel. Most of the time he had to paint while lying on his back! To simulate this experience have the students tape a sheet of drawing paper to the undersides of their desks. Tell them to lay on the floor underneath their desks so they can reach up to paint a picture. Brave students may want to try using watercolors or tempera paints from this position, but marker or crayons would also be acceptable.

Making Models

Here are some easy recipes for making models. The ingredients are inexpensive and readily available. Plus, students will have fun creating these projects.

Globes

Materials: balloons; flour; water; bowls or empty margarine tubs; newspaper, torn into strips; tempera paint; paintbrushes; colored markers; straight pins (to pop balloons)
Directions:
- Blow up a balloon and tie with a knot.
- Mix 2 measures of flour to 1 measure of water in the margarine tubs to make a thick paste.
- Dip strips of paper into paste and spread them over the balloon until it's completely covered. (Only the tied-off end should be showing.)
- Repeat the above step so that the balloon is covered with two layers of paper.
- Allow plenty of time to dry before popping the balloon; gently remove the balloon and patch the hole with additional strips of paper. Allow to dry.
- Paint the entire surface of the balloon with tempera; allow time to dry.
- When dry, use markers to show the equator, prime meridian, North Pole, South Pole, and lines of longitude and latitude.

Volcanoes

Materials: flour; salt; saucepan; cream of tartar; food coloring; cooking oil; wooden spoon; one-cup measuring cup; teaspoon; tablespoon; hot plate or stove top
Directions:
- Mix two cups of flour with one cup of salt in the saucepan.
- Add a few drops of brown food coloring, four teaspoons of cream of tartar, and two tablespoons of cooking oil to the mixture in the sauce pan.
- Stir constantly over low heat until the dough thickens.
- Make another batch of dough in the same manner using orange food coloring instead of brown.
- After the dough cools, mold a volcano with the brown dough; make an indentation in the top.
- Add some orange dough around the sides of the volcano to simulate running lava; allow plenty of time to dry. See page 26 for a way to simulate a lava flow.

Oceans

Materials: plaster of Paris; water; straws; plywood or heavy cardboard; poster paints, paintbrushes; pan

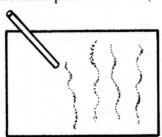

Directions:
- Mix the plaster of Paris and water in the pan.
- Pour onto the cardboard or plywood. Caution: Do not pour the mixture into the sink or toilet.
- With the straw blow gently over the surface to form waves; work quickly.
- After drying, paint your ocean.

Quick Check

Assignment

Name	1	2	3	4	5	6	7	8	9	10	11	12	13	14	15	16

✔ = completed

Extensions and Follow-Ups

The following list is a compilation of ideas and activities that can be used as extensions or follow-ups to some of the projects outlined in this book. While some of the ideas below may not be accessible or available to you, alternate methods can be improvised. Any of these activities may be adjusted and changed to suit your classroom needs.

Maritime Museum: Visit a maritime museum, particularly one that has ancient and modern nautical instruments and pictures or models of old ships.

Planetarium: Many colleges and universities have a planetarium on campus. Arrange for a classroom trip to see the stars and planets. An evening or weekend visit may have to be planned.

Model Ships: Have the students work in groups to build model ships. Hobby shops will have all the necessary supplies, including odorless airplane glue.

Geography Games: Improve students' geography skills with Texas Instruments' **Passport to the World Geography Game.** Players are guided by an electronic flight controller and asked questions that cover climate, countries, famous people, food, clothing, and more. Two other geography games include *GeoSafari* from Educational Insights and *Where in the World?* from Earth Care Paper, Inc. (P.O. Box 7070 Madison, WI 53707).

Books: Supplement the main selection, *The Log of Christopher Columbus' First Voyage to America,* with a book that provides the details that are missing: *Christopher Columbus: Voyage to the Unknown* by Nancy Smiler Levinson (Lodestar Books, 1990).

Space Center: Visit a space center (not widely available). To learn how students can go to Space Camp, call this toll-free number: 1-800-63SPACE. Write to NASA, Goddard Space Flight Center, Mail Code 130.3, Greenbelt, Maryland, 20771 for a list of free and inexpensive materials.

Guest Speakers: Contact a university, historical society, or library to find people who are very knowledgeable on a pertinent topic. Invite them to speak to your class.

Art: Visit local museums or art studios which display 16th century art. If unavailable, use some ideas and projects from *The Metropolitan Museum Art Activity Book* by Osa Brown (1983).

Cooking: Prepare Spanish, Aztec, Portuguese, and/or Italian food. Eat some of the foods that the Native Americans first shared with Columbus.

Software: One of the hottest video games around leads the player on an educational journey through 45 countries. *Where in the World Is Carmen Sandiego?* by Broderbund is a fun way to learn geography. (Also in book form—see Bibliography, page 80.)

An Explorers' Bulletin Board

Purpose: This interactive bulletin board is to be used as a means of introducing, drilling, and reviewing exploration terms, vocabulary, and concepts.

Materials: blue and green butcher paper; stapler; scissors; brown construction paper; tagboard, small envelopes; 3" x 5" index cards

Construction:

- Line the bulletin board with blue butcher paper; staple to bulletin board surface.
- Cut a simple wave with green butcher paper (see diagram above); staple to background.
- Reproduce the patterns (page 74, 75, and 76) on white construction paper and then color the ship patterns brown; cut out.
- Assemble and attach all patterns to the bulletin board background.
- Staple an envelope—opening side towards the front—onto each ship.
- Label the index cards with vocabulary words, exploration terms, or other assignments; store in one envelope.
- Label a matching set of index cards with corresponding answers; store in the other envelope.
- Write the word EXPLORERS on a section of tagboard; staple to the bulletin board background.

Directions:

- Student pairs can practice together. One reads a question and the other one finds the answer. Have them alternate reading and answering questions.
- Fill the envelope with creative writing topics or research projects; give students their choice of assignments. (Sample writing topics can be found on page 48; research projects on pages 37-39 and 47.)

An Explorers' Bulletin Board *(cont.)*

Ship's Aft

(make 2)

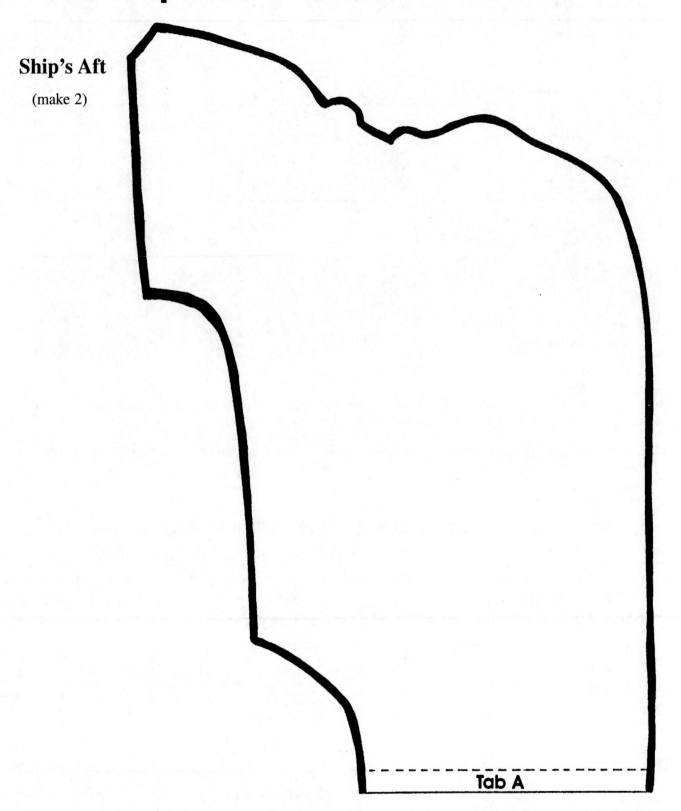

Tab A

An Explorers' Bulletin Board *(cont.)*

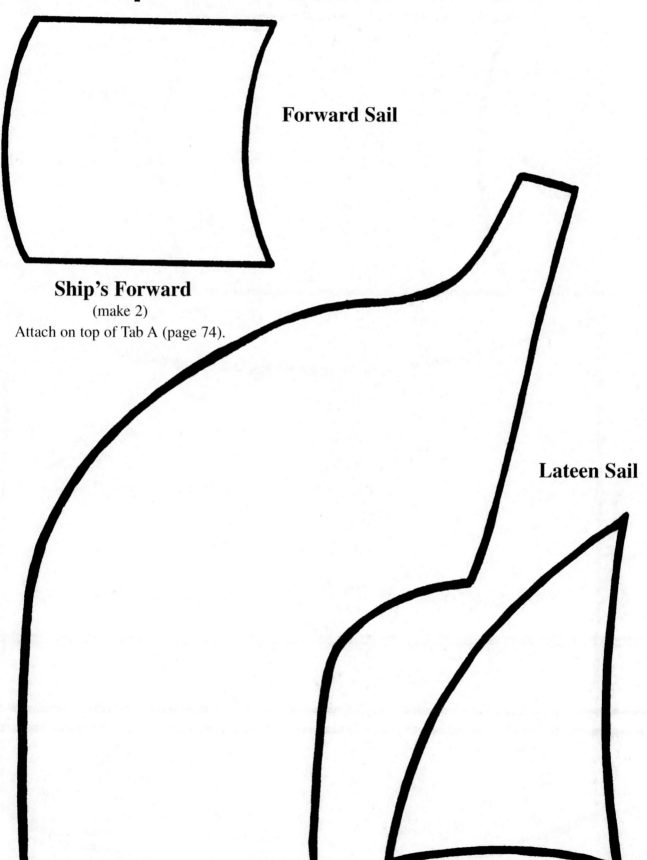

Forward Sail

Ship's Forward
(make 2)
Attach on top of Tab A (page 74).

Lateen Sail

An Explorers' Bulletin Board *(cont.)*

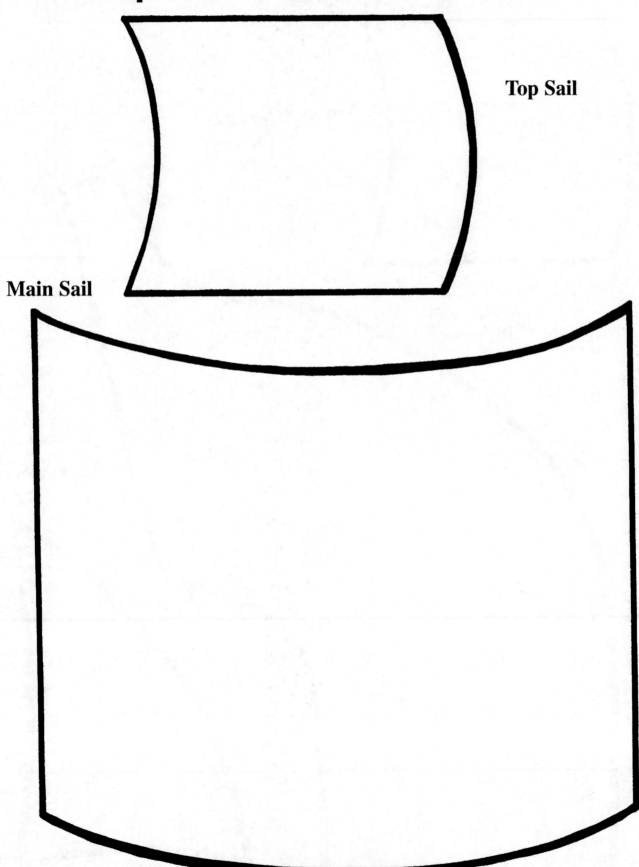

Top Sail

Main Sail

Answer Key

Page 10
1. cross-staff
2. compass
3. lateen
4. rudder
5. astrolabe
6. carrack
7. ampoletta

Page 11
1. Palos, Spain
2. league
3. Christopher Columbus
4. 10,000 maradevis
5. man-of-war bird
6. Teneriffe
7. Martin Alonzo Pinzon
8. flying fish
9. *Pinta*
10. dories
11. tree trunks
12. red caps
13. tern
14. crab
15. parrots

Page 13

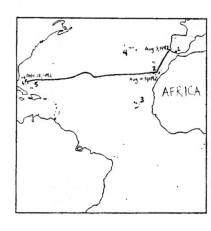

1. Palos, Spain
2. Canary Islands
4. Azores Islands
5. Bahama Islands

Page 15
1. Carved fragments of wood from the West; the finding of large reeds which did not grow in western Europe or Africa; covered boats and men's bodies which had washed up on shore. (See page near front of book entitled Evidences of Land in the West.)
2. They dreaded going on the voyage and hoped the damage would force Columbus to turn back.
3. He did not want to alarm the men since they were afraid to be far from shore.
4. The men thought these signs meant they were close to land.
5. He wanted to convert the people to Christianity, and to find a westerly route to India.
6. They needed wind to sail; they were afraid they'd never reach land or return home.
7. Columbus didn't want the men to become discouraged if they saw how long the journey was.
8. To jump off the ship into the waters below.
9. Wind power was necessary to sail the ships.
10. The first to see land would claim a prize.
11. They followed the flight of birds.
12. By reminding them of the advantages they might gain from it.
13. To gain their trust.
14. Because they were naked.
15. He wanted them to learn his language
16. He felt the natives needed the cotton and didn't want to take advantage of them.
17. He felt it was part of his duty.
18. A volcano.
19. Triangular shaped sails
20. A shooting star.
21. A sign of being near land.
22. They thought whales always kept near the coast
23. The crew had mistakenly thought that this was true and so became alarmed at the idea.

Page 15 (*cont.*)
24. They force other birds to disgorge what they've swallowed and then they eat it.
25. The Native Americans gasped when they were shown a sword, and they cut themselves on the blade.
26. Through sign language.
27. They were neither black nor white.
28. Because they were very friendly and they appeared to have no religion.

Page 16

Demanding:	The men . . .
Stubborn:	Columbus refused . . .
Adventurous:	Columbus dared . . .
Thorough:	Columbus kept . . .
Encouraging:	When the men . . .
Confident	He felt sure that . . .
Observant:	He took . . .
Untruthful:	Fewer leagues . . .

Page 19
I Friday, August 3: 15
   Sunday, August 5: 40
   Monday, August 6: 29
   Tuesday, August 7: 25
1. Sunday
2. Friday
3. 109
4. 27
5. Monday
II
1. 2
2. 12
3. 12
III
1. 123 leagues
2. first sentence
IV 71;1704

Page 20
1. 90
2. 540
3. $100
4. $1000
5. $10
6. 5,000 miles
7. 166.38
8. 55
9. 9
10. 24

Answer Key *(cont.)*

Page 22

1. F   5. T   9. F
2. F   6. F   10. T
3. T   7. F   11. T
4. F   8. T   12. T

Page 23

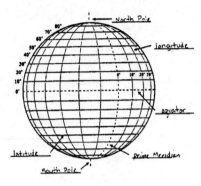

Page 28

I

Who: Christopher Columbus
What: set sail
When: Friday, August 3, 1492, 8 A.M.
Where: Palos, Spain
Why: to find a new route
How: by sailing west

II

Who: Captain Pinzon
What: reported the rudder
When: three days
Where: Canary Islands
Why: both men
How: Two sailors

III

Who: Admiral Columbus
What: sighted land
When: Friday, October 12, 1492, 2 A.M
Where: castle of the poop deck
Why: He was up high
How: He spotted a light

Page 35

6, 11, 3, 13, 8, 1, 9, 4, 12, 5, 10, 2, 14, 7

Page 42

Huitzilpochtli—Aztec sun god
Silk Road—trade route between China and the West
gauchos—Argentinean cowboys
outback—interior region of Australia
"the smoke that thunders"—Victoria Falls
"fool's gold"—iron pyrite
monsoon—seasonal winds
sagas—tales of Viking exploits
nomads—wandering people
bathysphere—spherical diving machine
dhow—type of ship used in Africa
Huns—fierce tribesman from central Asia
Llanos—dry, dusty plains
Skraelings—Norwegian name for Native Americans
"Cabo Tormentoso"- Cape of Storm
junks—15th century Chinese ships
scurvy—disease caused by lack of vitamin C
"Green Sea of Darkness"—an area at the Equator thought to be dangerous
caravel—Portuguese ship
Conquistador—spanish for conqueror
kayaks—one-man canoes
pampas—plains of Argentina
Sputnik I—the first satellite launched into space
knorr—Viking ship used for trading expeditions

Page 44

Burton:

at ease among the Arabs
spoke 29 languages
his legs become paralyzed
had written numerous books
appointed leader of the expedition

Both:

suffered from malaria
appointed by the Royal Geographic Society of London
ruthless and determined

Speke:

a quiet, careful planner
knew little Arabic
died in a shooting accident
led a 2nd expedition to Lake Victoria
took most of the credit for finding the Nile's source
named his discovery Lake Victoria
went deaf and blind

Page 45

wealthy
Native Americans
cocoa
tomatoes
diseases
smallpox
seventy-five
America
labor
tools
utensils
chickens

Page 49

1. 132, 000, 000 yards
2. 12
3. 12, 500 miles
4. 242
5. 201 km
6. 126 BC
7. 1200 bundles
8. 42; 2 left over
9. 480 km per year
10. 60/100; 3/5; 60%
11. 32, 400 miles
12. 20 hours

Answer Key *(cont.)*

Page 50

1. 3500	5. 415	9. 90
2. 14	6. 40	10. 12
3. 250	7. 62	11. 250
4. 38	8. 17	12. 80

Page 50

1. silver	6. sweet potatoes
2. nutmeg	7. pepper
3. tobacco	8. cinnamon
4. pineapples	9. silks
5. parrots	10. maize

Page 52

1. Spanish because it was metal.
2. Bright colors and metal spikes.
3. Cannons and horses.
4. 5. Answers may vary.

Page 57

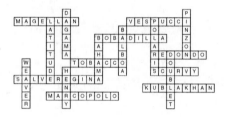

Page 59

Page 60

1. 6020
2. 24
3. 40
4. 3000

Page 61

Page 62

"That's one small step for a man, one giant leap for mankind."

Page 63

Comets
- tails are millions of miles long
- appear in the night sky for many days
- have a tail
- orbit around the sun
- hardly made of anything

Both
- are members of the solar system
- some are visible without telescope

Meteors
- are made of iron and atoms
- fall quickly to earth
- are called "shooting stars"

Page 64

1. Leonardo da Vinci
2. Henry VIII
3. Joann Gütenberg
4. Copernicus
5. Machiavelli
6. Michaelangelo
7. Mary Stuart
8. Ivan the Terrible
9. Martin Luther
10. Charles V

Page 65

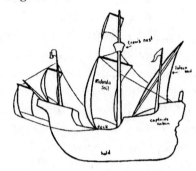

Page 66

Bibliography

Fiction

Litowinsky, Olga. *The High Voyage.* Delacorte, 1977.
Peel, John. *Where in the World Is Carmen Sandiego?* Western Publishing Company, 1991.
Roth, Susan L. *Marco Polo. His Notebook.* Doubleday, 1991.

Nonfiction

Anderson, Joan. *Christopher Columbus From Vision to Voyage.* Dial Books for Young Children, 1991.
Bourne, Russell. *The Big Golden Book of Christopher Columbus and Other Early Adventurers.* Western Publishing Company, 1991.
D'Aulaire, Edgar Parin and Ingri. *Columbus.* Doubleday, 1955.
Del Castillo, Bernard Diaz. *Cortes and the Conquest of Mexico.* Linnet Books, 1988.
Dyson, John. *Westward With Columbus.* Scholastic, 1991.
Everett, Felicity and Struan Reid. *The Usborne Book of Explorers.* Usborne Publishing Ltd., 1991.
Fradin, Dennis B. *Comets, Asteroids, and Meteors.* Childrens Press, 1984.
Fradin, Dennis. *Explorers.* Childrens Press, 1984.
Fritz, Jean. *Where Do You Think You're Going, Christopher Columbus?* Putnam, 1980.
Gerrard, Roy. *Sir Francis Drake: His Daring Deeds.* Farrar Straus & Giroux, 1988.
Greene, Carol. *Christopher Columbus.* Childrens Press, 1989.
Hargrove, Jim. *Ferdinand Magellan: First Around the World.* Childrens, 1990.
Hills, Ken. *The Voyage of Columbus.* Random House, 1991.
Humble, Richard. *The Voyage of Magellan.* Watts, 1989.
Israel, Elaine. *Years Over, Under, and Around: The New Explorers.* Gulf & Western Corp., 1980.
Lambert, David. *Earthquakes and Volcanoes.* Bookwright Press, 1988.
Las Casas, Bartholomew. *The Log of Christopher Columbus' First Voyage to America.* Shoe String Press, Hamden, CT, 06514.
Lawson, Robert. *I Discover Columbus.* Little, Brown & Co., 1969.
Levinson, Nancy Smiler. *Christopher Columbus: Voyager to the Unknown.* Lodestar Books, 1990.
Lye, Keith. *Explorers.* Silver, 1984.
Matthews, Rupert. *Explorer.* Alfred A. Knopf, 1991 (An Eyewitness Book).
Osborne, Mary Pope. *Christopher Columbus. Admiral of the Sea.* Dell, 1987.
Pearce, Q.L. *The Stargazer's Guide to the Galaxy.* RGA Publishing Group, 1991.
Roop, Peter and Connie, ed. *I Columbus. My Journal.* Avon Books, 1990.
Simon, Seymour. *Volcanoes.* Morrow Jr. Books, 1988.
Sullivan, George. *The Day We Walked on the Moon.* Scholastic, 1990.
Vautier, Ghislaine. *The Way of the Stars.* Cambridge University Press, 1982.

Reference

Guy, Arnold. *Datelines of World History.* Warwick Press, 1983.
Kandeatis, Christos. *The Junior Wall Chart of History.* Barnes and Noble, 1990.
Sandak, Cass R. *Explorers and Discovery.* Franklin Watts, 1983.

Teacher Created Materials

018   *Masterpiece of the Month*
137   *Newspaper Reporters*
138   *Newspapers*
161   *World Geography*

169   *Maps, Charts, Graphs, and Diagrams*
226   *Our Changing Earth*
343   *Connecting Geography and Literature*